A scene from the Second Stage Theatre production of "Dearly Departed." Set design by Allen Moyer.

DEARLY DEPARTED

A COMEDY
BY **DAVID BOTTRELL**
AND **JESSIE JONES**

★

**DRAMATISTS
PLAY SERVICE
INC.**

For Nick, Leigh, and Rob,
for their endless love and support

DEARLY DEPARTED was first presented at the Second Stage Theatre (Robyn Goodman, Carole Rothman, Artistic Directors), in New York City, on December 3, 1991. It was directed by Gloria Muzio; the set design was by Allen Moyer; the costume design was by Ellen McCartney; the lighting design was by Don Holder; the sound design was by Mark Bennett and the production stage manager was Stacey Fleischer. The cast was as follows:

BUD, RAY-BUD	Leo Burmester
RAYNELLE	Mary Fogarty
MARGUERITE	Sloane Shelton
ROYCE	Greg Germann
LUCILLE	Jessie Jones
SUZANNE	Linda Cook
JUNIOR	Dylan Baker
REVEREND HOOKER, CLYDE, NORVAL	J.R. Horn
DELIGHTFUL, NADINE	Wendy Lawless
VEDA, JUANITA	Jill Larson
THE JOY OF LIFE SINGERS	Mary Fogarty, Jill Larson, Sloane Shelton

DEARLY DEPARTED was performed in a workshop at the Long Wharf Theatre, in New Haven, Connecticut, in March, 1991. It was directed by Gloria Muzio and the stage manager was C.A. Clark. The cast was as follows:

BUD, JUNIOR	Brad Bellamy
RAYNELLE	Mary Fogarty
MARGUERITE	Sloane Shelton
ROYCE	William Hill
LUCILLE	Jessie Jones
RAY-BUD	Leo Burmester
SUZANNE	Susan Greenhill
REVEREND HOOKER, CLYDE, NORVAL	Ronn Carroll
DELIGHTFUL, NADINE	Kimberly Squires
VEDA, JUANITA	Karen MacDonald
THE JOY OF LIFE SINGERS	Mary Fogarty, Sloane Shelton, Karen MacDonald, William Hill

THE CHARACTERS

BUD TURPIN, an elderly man
RAYNELLE, his wife
RAY-BUD, their son
LUCILLE, his wife
JUNIOR, their other son
SUZANNE, his wife
MARGUERITE, Bud's sister
ROYCE, her son
DELIGHTFUL, Bud and Raynelle's only daughter
REVEREND HOOKER
VEDA, an elderly woman
NORVAL, her husband
NADINE, a young woman
CLYDE, a friend
JUANITA, a cousin by marriage
THE JOY OF LIFE SINGERS

THE SETTING

In and around the towns of Lula and Timson, somewhere below the Mason-Dixon Line. The time is the present.

DOUBLING THE CHARACTERS

The play was written to be performed by ten actors doubling in the roles. The following suggestions have worked well in the past:

Either JUNIOR or RAY-BUD doubles with BUD
REVEREND HOOKER doubles with NORVAL and CLYDE
DELIGHTFUL doubles with NADINE
JUANITA doubles with VEDA
Anybody other than JUNIOR or RAY-BUD can double as THE JOY OF LIFE SINGERS

5

REGARDING THE SET

In order to facilitate the numerous scene changes, we would suggest a simple unit set. The play was designed to work with minimal props, a few folding chairs, a kitchen table, a sofa (also used as Royce's bed in Act One) and a bed (in Act Two).

We would also like to go on record as strongly advising against using a real casket onstage.

DEARLY DEPARTED

ACT ONE

Scene 1

Bud and Raynelle, an elderly couple are seated in their kitchen. Bud seems lost in thought, a million miles away. Raynelle reads aloud from a letter. She reads in a plain matter of fact way.

RAYNELLE.
Dear Brother and Raynelle,

Well, Bud, I was expecting to see you at services Sunday, but I guess you thought you had something better to do. Again.

Well, you missed a good one. Our guest speaker, the Reverend Leon Streeber, gave a very interesting talk on some of the more obscure scriptures from Deuteronomy and Clarice Talbot's Sunday school class put on a real good puppet show based on the book of Ruth. Sure is a shame you missed it, but I guess there must have been something good on the T.V. I know how you like to watch that wrestling program. Wonder if they'll have a T.V. in Hell?

I don't know if I told you that I saw Norma Easterling in town last week for the first time since she defected to the Nazarines. As you might recall, I ended my friendship with Sister Easterling, after she disqualified three of my jars from last year's jelly judging, claiming they were not sealed properly. I am pleased to report that she is not nearly so uppity since

7

that nephew of hers went to the electric chair. She says she still chokes up every time she pays her light bill.

I noticed Retha Middleton was back working at the beauty shop again. She used to be one of Pauline's best girls, but has been having trouble getting customers since she lost that arm. Pauline says she thinks it just jangles the ladies when they see a one armed woman coming at 'em with a pair of scissors.

Ansil Kincaid's boy, Tiny, was over here mowing my grass and told me about Junior's business going belly up. When will that boy of yours learn? And speaking of heartache my own worthless son don't seem to be the least bit interested in finding another job. Ever since he got laid off from the sewage plant, he's fallen in with a real bad crowd.

I'll tell you, I think both our sons could learn a thing or two from Tiny. One thing about Tiny, that boy's a worker. He mowed the front yard, the side yard, the back yard, plus them six acres I've got out behind the house, restacked the firewood, cleaned out the garage, and hoed in the garden till it was too dark to see. Since his birthday is coming up next week, I gave him three dollars, instead of the usual two. It's hard to believe Tiny will be turning thirty-seven. They grow up so fast.

Well, that's about all the news for now. I've decided to come over and visit you next Sunday after services. One of you, and I'm not saying who, Bud, needs to get right with the Lord, and I'm just the lady for the job. We're gonna spend the whole day in prayer, discussing scripture, and singing hymns till we wear you down. Like it says in Second Peter 3:8 "One day is with the Lord as a thousand years."

Your sister,
Marguerite

(Raynelle closes the letter and turns to her husband.) Well, Bud, what do you think of that? *(Without moving a muscle, Bud tips over backward in his chair, disappearing from view. Raynelle slowly leans over and speaks to him.)* Bud? *(Pause.)* Bud? Are you feeling alright?

BLACKOUT

Scene 2

Royce's room at the boarding house and Marguerite's kitchen. Marguerite, with the phone to her ear, is wearing an apron and carries a large wooden spoon. Royce is sound asleep on his sofa bed that he has neglected to fold out, when his phone begins to ring. Right around the third ring, he manages to find the phone.

ROYCE.   Who the hell ... *(Finally answering.)* Hello.
MARGUERITE.   *(Singing at the top of her lungs.)* "Blessed Assurance! Jesus is mine! Oh, what a foretaste of glory divine!" *(Royce hangs up and rolls over. Marguerite re-dials.)* You're not getting out of it that easy. *(The phone rings three more times. Royce finally answers it. Marguerite picks up where she left off.)* "Heir of salvation! Purchase of love! Born of his spirit! Washed in his blood!"
ROYCE.   Good God, Mama.
MARGUERITE.   What was that? Was that blasphemy? Did I hear the Lord's name taken in vain?
ROYCE.   What time is it?
MARGUERITE.   7:00 A.M. "And the watchman said, The morning cometh and also the night: If you will inquire, inquire ye: Return, come." *(Pause.)*
ROYCE.   Uh huh.
MARGUERITE.   Isaiah 21:12.
ROYCE.   WHAT THE HELL DO YOU WANT??
MARGUERITE.   DON'T TALK FILTH! And what are you

doing still laying up in the bed at 7:00? Why aren't you out looking for a job? Are you suffering from a HANG-OVER? Did you spend all evening drinking and dancing and talking filth? Are you laid up there with some harlot?

ROYCE.   No, I'm not laid up with ...

MARGUERITE.   *(Whacking the phone receiver with her spoon.)* Harlot! Harlot! Can you hear me out there? Time to get up Harlot! Wake up, Harlot!

ROYCE.   Would you stop that! There ain't no harlot here for Gah ... *(He stops himself.)*

MARGUERITE.   Did I hear the Lord's name used again?

ROYCE.   No, you didn't. What do you want, Mama?

MARGUERITE.   Well, I guess a mother can't call up her lazy, good for nothing son just to see how he's doing.

ROYCE.   Well, why don't you ask me how I'm doing, so I can go back to sleep.

MARGUERITE.   I haven't got time to listen to your problems. I've got too much to do. Your uncle Bud passed this morning.

ROYCE.   Good God.

MARGUERITE.   That's three. That's three G.O.D.'s and it's only 7:05 in the morning.

ROYCE.   What'd he die of?

MARGUERITE.   Stroke. No surprise. Been hanging by a thread for years.

ROYCE.   *(Lighting a cigarette.)* Well, I'm real sorry to hear that.

MARGUERITE.   You want to know what I'm sorry about? Your uncle Bud didn't belong to any church whatsoever. Always scorned and mocked the doings of good Christian people. And you know what that means don't you?

ROYCE.   Don't say it, Mama.

MARGUERITE.   Roasting on the end of a pitchfork, even as we speak.

ROYCE.   Mama, it's awful early ...

MARGUERITE.   Cryin' out in eternal torment.

ROYCE.   Mama.

MARGUERITE.   Flesh torn by demons.

ROYCE. *(Shouting.)* How's Aunt Raynelle! You remember Aunt Raynelle? The widow? How's she doing?

MARGUERITE. How do you think she's doing? Her husband just dropped dead right there at the breakfast table. Awful. She's doing awful. That's why we got to get over there and offer her comfort and Christian counsel.

ROYCE. What do you mean "we"?

MARGUERITE. Are you telling me you're gonna turn your back on your family in this time of tragedy?

ROYCE. Can't Ray-Bud and them come and get you?

MARGUERITE. No, they can't. They've got too much to do. And besides I'd die of shame if they knew my own son wouldn't come over here and drive me over to my only brother's grieving widow. Or maybe you'd like me to walk the twenty miles over to Lula and it 110 in the shade today? Maybe you'd like me to drop dead from heat stroke?

ROYCE. What time do you want to go?

MARGUERITE. When do you think I want to go? Next month? Now! Get your lazy worthless self out of bed and take me over there now. Bud's not gonna keep long in this heat. *(She hangs up and exits.)*

ROYCE. Bye Mama. I love you too. *(He hangs up, rolls over and pulls the covers over his head.)*

BLACKOUT

Scene 3

Lucille and Ray-Bud in their kitchen. Lucille is talking on the phone. Ray-Bud is sipping coffee.

LUCILLE. *(Frantically writing notes.)* Okay, okay, Merline. Either Ray-Bud or I will be down this afternoon to pick up those brochures. You bet. Well, I sure appreciate that. Now we were planning on using the community room for the visitation tomorrow night starting about seven. And we're expecting quite a crowd so you better tell Cecil to pull out those extra folding chairs. Oh, I didn't know there was an extra charge for that. Well, I'm sure that won't be a problem. *(Ray-Bud clears his throat.)* Now there'll probably be quite a bit of food, so we'll be needing those long tables y'all had out for the Crenshaw funeral. Oh really? *(She glances over at Ray-Bud, then turns away and whispers into the phone.)* How much? *(Ray-Bud clears his throat again.)* Well, okay. Now, we're planning on having the service Friday about eleven and then head out for the cemetery around noon. Right now, I'm assuming Ray-Bud's mother and sister will probably be riding in the hearse with the body and we'll.... Oh, I see. Well, I just assumed.... Well what if one of us drove it? Ray-Bud's a real good driver. Oh, of course, your insurance and all.

RAY-BUD.   *(Loudly.)* Tell her we'll just strap him on top of the Impala!

LUCILLE.   *(Deeply embarrassed.)* Oh no, honey. That was ... that was just the T.V. *(Calling off.)* "Ray-Bud, turn down that T.V.! I'm trying to make your Daddy's funeral arrangements in here!" I'm so sorry, Merline. Now, where were we? Oh, of course, I understand. Yes, I know Cecil has to make a living. I'm sure he's a wonderful driver. Listen, honey, I've got to get going here. Ray-Bud hasn't even had breakfast yet. I'll see you this afternoon and we'll work out the rest of the details then. Okay ... okay ... okay. Thanks, Merline. *(She hangs up.)*

RAY-BUD.   What the hell are you thanking her for? Damn thieves!

LUCILLE.   Now, Ray-Bud.

RAY-BUD.   Who ever thought up the word "grave-robber" must have had one of Cecil and Merline's calendars hanging on their wall.

LUCILLE.   Now, Ray.

RAY-BUD.   *(Nervously pacing.)* And what's my Daddy doing down at Depew's anyway. That's what I'd like to know? The Turpins have always gone to Patterson's.

LUCILLE.   Well, I thought that was sort of strange too, but Depew's is what your Mama wanted.

RAY-BUD.   Revenge! That's what it is, Lucille!

LUCILLE. What are you talking about?

RAY-BUD. Cold blooded revenge. After all these years he's got me. He's got me by the throat!

LUCILLE. Who's got you?

RAY-BUD. Cecil Depew! Don't you remember when Cecil peed his pants in the fourth grade! "P.U. HERE COME DEPEW!" I started it! I started it, and it followed him all the way through high school!

LUCILLE. Ray, you got to get ahold of yourself.

RAY-BUD. I should've known it! I should've seen it coming! When the rest of us was out shooting birds with B.B. guns, Cecil was running around burying 'em in shoe boxes. He's gonna nickel and dime me to death!

LUCILLE. *(Trying to get ahold of him.)* Ray!

RAY-BUD. He's gonna break me!

LUCILLE. Ray! Ray, you got to calm down. Now, listen to me, Honey. Depew's is your mama's choice and we just have to respect it. I know this is a hard time. I know how much you loved your Daddy. Why I loved him too. He and your mama were always so sweet to me. They never failed to send me a card after every one of my miscarriages. And I remember how Daddy Bud would always write the same sweet thing: "Better Luck Next Time."

RAY-BUD. I don't know how I'm gonna get through this, Lucille. I swear to God, I don't. I hate funerals. I hate everything about 'em.

LUCILLE. Now we're a family and we're all gonna hang together. And speaking of family, your Aunt Marguerite has volunteered to spend the night with your mama. And Junior, Suzanne, and the kids can stay here with us.

RAY-BUD. They're not staying here, Lucille.

LUCILLE. Ray-Bud! He's your brother!

RAY-BUD. They can shack up down at the Motel 6. I'm not having Junior and that mess in here.

LUCILLE. Ray, you know they can't afford a motel.

RAY-BUD. Is that my fault? Did I hold a gun to his head and tell him to mortgage his house and blow all his money on that pipe dream? Junior, a businessman? Junior couldn't sell lemonade in Hell, Lucille.

LUCILLE.   He tried so hard, Ray.

RAY-BUD.   Face it, Lucille. He's an idiot, and I'm not having him in here. I'm not gonna sit here and listen to Suzanne running her mouth and I believe them children are demon possessed.

LUCILLE.   They're sweet people, Ray. They've just had a little string of hard luck lately.

RAY-BUD.   Demon possessed, Lucille. Mark my words.

LUCILLE.   *(Handing him his sack lunch.)* We'll talk about it tonight. You're gonna be late. Clyde says they got three transmissions backed up there waiting for you. And don't forget you got to stop by the shoe store. Size 10-D.

RAY-BUD.   I'll remember.

LUCILLE.   And Ray.... We're not gonna have any "problems" are we?

RAY-BUD.   No, Lucille, we're not gonna have any "problems." Just do me one favor. When I die, don't tell nobody. Just bury me in the backyard and tell everybody I left you.

BLACKOUT

Scene 4

Junior and Suzanne in the car. They drive in silence. Suzanne is looking over some sheet music.

SUZANNE.   How's she gonna go on? That's what I'd like to know. How's she gonna face life without Daddy Bud? I just don't know how she's gonna go on without losing her mind. *(She waits for a response but doesn't get one.)* Well, I can't decide what to sing. Of course, I don't know how I'll get through it. I swear to God, I don't. I'll probably just fall down on the floor in a big pool of tears. God knows nobody would blame me if I did. All our humiliation and now Daddy Bud has to up and die without seeing you make something of yourself.

JUNIOR.   Maybe you could sing "Jesus on the Cross."

SUZANNE.   I don't know. That doesn't seem sad enough for a funeral. And God knows it's gonna be sad to be sitting there thinking that your Daddy died knowing we had to sell everything we owned and move into that God-awful trailer just to pay off that big dream of yours.

JUNIOR.   Maybe you could set *that* to music, Suzanne.

SUZANNE.   I believe I was just stating the facts, wasn't I? You know I loved him too, Junior. He was just like my own Daddy. I was the one that had to go crawling to him like a snake and beg for the money to buy shoes for our children, you know. But I did it. I humbled myself. And do you know why I did it, Junior? It can all be summed up in two little words: "For Love." *(Suddenly slapping "the children" over the backseat.)* I TOLD YOU TO QUIT KICKING THE BACK OF MY SEAT! I know you're hungry! You think I'm not! It'd be nice to stop and get something to eat wouldn't it? Well, maybe we could if your Daddy hadn't lost all our money! *(Back to Junior.)* Love, Junior. That's been the curse of my life. And now we have to face your family with all of them knowing. All of them looking down at us. Laughing at us. Who ever heard of a machine that cleans parking lots?

JUNIOR.   That'll do, Suzanne.

SUZANNE.   All our money down the toilet, Junior. How do you feel about that? You think I like working at Newberry's? Slaving to keep that wax fruit section looking nice. You think I wouldn't love to stay home and watch soap operas all day like my good for nothing sisters do. That would suit me fine, mister. Let me tell you that right now. I don't want to work, I have to. I'd love to stay home and keep a decent house, cook for you, maybe learn to sew and make some clothes for the children. That's all I ever wanted to be was just a good wife and mother. *(Suddenly slapping "the children" again.)* YOU DO THAT AGAIN AND I'M GONNA TELL YOUR DADDY TO PULL THIS CAR OVER AND THROW YOU ALL OUT IN THE ROAD! How would you like us to just put you out in the road, and drive off and never look back? Then what would you do with no mother and daddy to look after you?

Starve! Starve to death in the road! *(She settles back in her seat, returns to her music.)* Go on and cry, you big babies.

JUNIOR. *(Over his shoulder, quietly.)* Y'all know your Mama loves you. She was just kidding.

SUZANNE. We'll see who's kidding? Don't miss this turn off. I just don't know how they expect me to stand up there and sing. I don't know how I'll do it.

JUNIOR. I'm sure you'll do your best.

SUZANNE. My best? That's a good one. You don't know a thing about it, Junior. In order to do my best, I'd have to have confidence. I used to have confidence. I could have been a professional. I had the talent. I could have married your cousin, Teddy-Wayne, and been the wife of a lawyer. Had a big house with a swimming pool. But no, I couldn't think of myself. That's been my curse my whole life. I never once thought of myself. I had to listen to my foolish heart and get married to a dreamer. A beautiful dreamer who goes out and blows all our money on a big piece of machinery to clean parking lots.

JUNIOR. You're pushing it.

SUZANNE. Did you ever once stop to think that maybe nobody gave a damn about a clean parking lot.

JUNIOR. You're really pushing it.

SUZANNE. And of course, it came as a big surprise to you when everybody just laughed in your face when you asked them if they wanted their parking lot cleaned.

JUNIOR. I'm gonna kill us, Suzanne.

SUZANNE. Don't make me laugh. *(Junior starts swerving the car back and forth across the road.)*

JUNIOR. *(Overlapping.)* I'M GONNA KILL US! I'M GONNA KILL US! I'M GONNA KILL US! I'M GONNA KILL US!

SUZANNE. *(Overlapping.)* STOP IT! STOP IT, JUNIOR! STOP IT! STOP IT! *(Junior slams on the brakes, reaches under the seat and produces a gun.)*

JUNIOR. SHUT UP! SHUT UP! SHUT UP! I've had it, Suzanne! I'm at the end of my goddamn rope! I can't take it anymore! My Daddy just died! Can you understand that? Can you hear me? Am I getting through that thick skull of yours?

My Daddy just died. I'm thirty-five years old, I'm dead ass broke, I've got no job, no prospects, three kids and worst of all, I'm married to you! Now, shut up! Just shut up! I want some peace, you hear me! You say one more word about parking lots and I swear to God, I'll kill you and me too! You got that? *(Pause.)*

SUZANNE.   Tense, tense, tense. You are so tense. Put that away. *(She goes back to her music. He puts away the gun, starts the car, and pulls out on the road. Over her shoulder, quietly.)* Your Daddy wasn't really gonna kill me. He was just kidding. Y'all know your Daddy and I love each other. Buddy, what have you got in your mouth? *(She reaches out her hand.)* Spit that out! Don't pick things up off the floor of the car. You don't know what kind of filth it's got on it. *(She rolls down the window and starts to throw the object out, when she notices what it is.)* Junior?

JUNIOR.   What?

SUZANNE.   Do you know what this is?

JUNIOR.   No.

SUZANNE.   It's a woman's earring.

BLACKOUT

Scene 5

Raynelle, Reverend Hooker and Raynelle's obese daughter are seated in Raynelle's kitchen. The daughter is eating potato chips.

RAYNELLE.   Can I get you a little more coffee, Reverend Hooker?

REVEREND.   No, Sister Turpin, I'm fine. You just rest yourself. I know this has been an awful day for you.

RAYNELLE.   Yes, it has.

REVEREND.   It must be a blessing to have your daughter living here with you at this time of bereavement.

RAYNELLE. Yes, it is. I believe you've met my daughter, Delightful.

REVEREND. Yes, I believe I have. I know this must have been an awful shock to you too. How're you doing, Delightful?

DELIGHTFUL. *(Still eating.)* Okay.

REVEREND. Well, she's a blessing.

RAYNELLE. Yes, she is. *(Pause; they both watch Delightful eat for a moment.)* Our youngest. Sort of a surprise, late in life.

REVEREND. A comfort to you in your old age.

RAYNELLE. She's precious to me.

REVEREND. I can see why. *(They both watch Delightful eat again. Reverend Hooker takes out his pen.)* Well, Sister, as you know, Brother Bud was not a regular member of the church, but I knew you'd want me to say a few words at the service, so I was hoping you might be able to tell me a little something about your late husband that I might be able to include in my remarks. Now, just in your own words, what kind of man was Brother Bud?

RAYNELLE. Well, he was mean.

REVEREND. Mean.

RAYNELLE. Mean as a snake.

REVEREND. I see.

RAYNELLE. And surly.

REVEREND. Surly.

RAYNELLE. Right surly.

REVEREND. *(Writing.)* Right surly.

RAYNELLE. Yeah.

REVEREND. And how many years were you and Brother Turpin married?

RAYNELLE. Thirty-nine years.

REVEREND. *(Writing.)* Thirty-nine years.

RAYNELLE. Thirty-nine long ones, Reverend.

REVEREND. I see. Sister, I did not know Brother Turpin well, but to me he seemed a quiet man. A man of inner strength. A man who knew his own mind, kept his own counsel, and was at peace with the world. A man of few words with a strong sense of family and community. A good neighbor you could go to if you needed a helping hand. A good husband and father. A man who was close to the earth. A wise, noble and gentle man. *(He pauses to see how this is going over with Raynelle.)*

RAYNELLE.   That's cause you didn't know him till he was old and sick. He was mean and right surly.

REVEREND.   Sister, in my experience it's best to remember the happier times.

RAYNELLE.   Few and far between, Reverend.

REVEREND.   I see.

RAYNELLE.   You see, Reverend Hooker, after Ray-Bud and Junior were born, I got interested in going back to services. Bud and I were both raised in the church, but we were young and had drifted somewhat from the shore. Well, I started going back pretty regular with Bud's sister, Marguerite. And one night, during a revival preached by the Reverend Reesie Campbell, who was our pastor here for many years before you came, I got saved. Well, when I came home and announced that to Bud, he just about hit the ceiling. You never heard such a stream of filthy language in your life. So I said to him "Your mortal soul is in grave danger, Buddy Boy and if you've got a brain to an acre, you'll go down there and get yourself saved before it's too late." Well, he wouldn't have none of it, so I said to him, "If that's the way you feel about it, mister, I'm cutting you off."

REVEREND.   I beg your pardon?

RAYNELLE.   Not so much as a warm handshake for thirty-three years, Reverend. I guess you might say we had sort of a stand off. Well, except for that one time. *(They both look at Delightful, who is emptying the last crumbs from the sack into her mouth.)*

REVEREND.   I see. Did Brother Turpin ever come to embrace the Church?

RAYNELLE.   Not that I know of.

REVEREND.   Well, don't you fret, Sister. We don't know what transactions the Lord makes with a soul in those last few moments on this earth.

RAYNELLE.   Well, if the Lord made a transaction with Bud,

it must have been a quick one cause he was dead by the time he hit the floor.

REVEREND. Well, we don't know that for sure, do we Sister?

RAYNELLE. Looked dead to me.

REVEREND. *(Putting his notes away.)* Well, I believe I've got all the information I need. I'll just be on my way. I'm sure you've got family coming and all. Is Brother Bud resting down at Patterson's?

RAYNELLE. No, we've got him down at Depew's. Little cheaper.

REVEREND. Now don't you worry, Sister Turpin, I believe I'll be able to come up with a suitable eulogy for your husband. Delightful, is there anything you'd like to add? *(Delightful lets out a huge belch and shakes her head.)*

RAYNELLE. Guess that about does it, Reverend.

BLACKOUT

Scene 6

Marguerite and Royce sit in his car. There is a long silence. Royce looks over his shoulder, then checks his watch.

MARGUERITE. I can not believe you ran out of gas.

ROYCE. Well, I did.

MARGUERITE. I can not believe it. Today of all days. My only brother laying in the funeral home. The entire family waiting for us. And here we sit on Route 35, in the middle of nowhere, in this death trap you call a car and not a speck of gas in it. You did this on purpose, didn't you?

ROYCE. Ray-Bud'll be here soon. It's been over a half hour since I called him. Said he'd come as soon as he could.

MARGUERITE. What time is it?

ROYCE. 'Bout five.

MARGUERITE. I can not believe it.

ROYCE. Believe it, alright! Just believe it!

MARGUERITE. You do these things to torture me, don't you?

ROYCE. Yeah, Mama. I siphoned out that gas just so you and I could spend a little more time together.

MARGUERITE. You're a demon, Royce. I swear to God, you're the devil incarnate.

ROYCE. Look, just keep your drawers on, alright. Ray-Bud'll be here soon as he can. And believe me, he can't get here soon enough to suit me. So let's just sit here and be quiet for a while. *(Pause.)*

MARGUERITE. So, we're just gonna sit here.

ROYCE. Yep, that's the plan. *(They sit in silence for a moment. Royce turns the ignition, and then reaches down and turns on the radio. It is tuned in to his favorite station which is playing a raunchy, honky tonk song. After a moment, Marguerite leans over and changes the station to a contemporary Christian station. After another moment, Royce changes it back. Marguerite changes it back. It becomes a rapid battle with each person determined to keep it on the station of their choice. Suddenly, the knob comes off in Marguerite's hand.)*

MARGUERITE. Ha! Ha! Jesus got the knob! *(She drops it down the front of her dress.)*

ROYCE. That's okay, Mama, cause Satan's got the car keys. *(He turns the ignition and the radio goes dead. He laughs maniacally.)*

MARGUERITE. I can not believe you're my son. You got Beelzebub in you, boy. What happened to you, Royce? Why did you turn out so evil?

ROYCE. Just lucky, I guess.

MARGUERITE. To think I was in labor seventeen hours with you. Seventeen hours of unbelievable torment.

ROYCE. Mama.

MARGUERITE. Screaming out in unbearable agony.

ROYCE. Mama, don't get started in on ...

MARGUERITE. They offered me drugs to ease my suffering, but I turned 'em down. Said, "No, I don't want your dope to ease my misery. I'll gladly bear the torment to give life to my child."

ROYCE.   Mama.

MARGUERITE.   "Just give me a bullet to bite on," I told
'em. "If our Lord and Savior could be nailed to a cross and
still forgive his persecutors, then surely I can forgive this child
for busting my guts." If I'd known then how it was all gonna
turn out, I'd have told them to shoot me right there on the
table.

ROYCE.   Remind me and I'll buy you a pistol for Mother's
Day.

MARGUERITE.   You're not gonna turn out like your brother,
are you? I think we can safely say Jim-Ed won't be coming
back to town for your Uncle Bud's funeral.

ROYCE.   Leave Jim-Ed alone, Mama.

MARGUERITE.   What are you gonna do, Royce? That's what
I'd like to know. What do you plan on doing with yourself?
Them unemployment checks aren't gonna last forever, you
know. Have you thought about that? About the future? You
better learn what's important. Life is not drinking and dancing and loose women. Life is not a good time, Royce.

ROYCE.   Well, you're living proof of that.

MARGUERITE.   You better straighten up and fly right, boy,
or you'll be doing your dancing on a bed of flamin' hot coals.
You better make a plan for yourself and make it soon.

ROYCE.   I got a plan.

MARGUERITE.   Well, let's hear it. Time's running out,
Royce.

ROYCE.   Well, when them unemployment checks run out,
I'm gonna marry some woman and have a kid, so I can get
on welfare. (Pause.)

MARGUERITE.   That's your plan.

ROYCE.   Yeah, that's pretty much it.

MARGUERITE.   Well, I just got one thing to say to that.

ROYCE.   Yeah, what?

MARGUERITE.   "Blessed Assurance! Jesus is mine! Oh, what
a foretaste of glory divine!" (After a moment, Royce, deciding it is
better to sing than to listen, joins her in the song. The lights fade on
them as they sing at the top of their lungs.)

Scene 7

Raynelle, Marguerite, Royce, Delightful, and Ray-Bud are seated in Ray-Bud's living room. All are looking over and passing around brochures.

RAY-BUD.   Well, Mama, do you see anything there that strikes your fancy?

RAYNELLE.   Who knew there were so many different kinds of caskets.

ROYCE.   I like "The Sportsman."

MARGUERITE.   Who asked you, Satan? This is Raynelle's decision.

RAYNELLE.   Well, yeah that one's nice. *(Lucille enters carrying a tray of corn dogs.)* There'll all nice. It don't really matter.

MARGUERITE.   What do you mean it don't matter? Of course it matters. You want to put him in pine box?

LUCILLE.   Oh, of course, she doesn't. *(Offering corn dogs.)* Corn dog, Mama Ray?

RAYNELLE.   Thank you, Lucille. *(Takes one.)*

LUCILLE.   I thought "The Diplomat" was awfully nice.

RAYNELLE.   Yeah, that looks good.

LUCILLE.   Looks real sturdy. *(Junior enters and everyone falls silent for a moment.)* Well, how's Suzanne feeling, Junior?

JUNIOR.   Oh, she's doing a little bit better, I guess. She just gets these sick headaches sometimes.

LUCILLE.   Oh, how awful. Corn dog, Junior?

JUNIOR.   Thank you, Lucille. So y'all decide anything?

RAY-BUD.   No, Mama's just looking over a few models.

RAYNELLE.   It's so hard to choose. What do you think, Junior?

JUNIOR.   Well, I think we ought to go with "The Gentleman Farmer."

RAY-BUD.   You do, huh?

RAYNELLE.   That's real pretty, isn't it, Ray?

RAY-BUD.   Seems kinda pricey to me.

RAYNELLE.   Well, maybe you're right.

JUNIOR. *(Moving over to sit next to Raynelle.)* No, no, no. I don't want you thinking like that. This was our one and only Daddy, and we're gonna do everything the right way. We're not gonna worry about money at a time like this. I went down to Depew's this afternoon and told Cecil we wanted everything first class all the way. No skimping on the flowers or nothing. Money was no object. *(Ray-Bud clears his throat.)*

LUCILLE. Ray-Bud would you help me in the kitchen for a minute?

RAY-BUD. No, I think I'd like to hear Junior's thoughts on all this. Go on, Junior. What were you saying?

JUNIOR. I was just saying how Mama shouldn't worry about any of this. We'll take care of everything. And we're not even gonna think about what it costs. This is what family is for, Mama. When Daddy makes that final trip up the hill to the family plot, and we're all standing there saying our last goodbyes, we will be able to hold our heads up high, and say we did our best. We went the extra mile. We gave till it hurt. He would have not done less for any of us, and we all know that's the truth. This is a time to remember, that someday, each of us, in turn, will be making that lonesome journey to our final resting place.

RAY-BUD. Some of us might be getting there sooner than we think, Junior. *(Suzanne enters. She holds an ice pack to her temple.)*

LUCILLE. Well, hello, Suzanne. How're you feeling, Honey?

SUZANNE. *(Weakly.)* Oh, a little bit better, I guess. Are the children driving you crazy?

LUCILLE. No, Honey, we locked them out of the house.

SUZANNE. Well, good. Lucille, can I borrow one of your nerve pills? I left mine at home.

LUCILLE. Oh sure, Honey. I'll be right back. *(Exits.)*

JUNIOR. *(Helping Suzanne to sit next to Raynelle.)* You shouldn't be standing up, Precious. Come in here and sit down. Would you like a corn dog, Baby? *(Holding one up to her mouth.)* Might make you feel better. Choo-choo here comes the train.

SUZANNE. *(Gently pushing it away.)* No, as much as I'd like to, I just know I'd vomit it up.

RAYNELLE. I'm sorry you're feeling so bad, Suzanne.

SUZANNE. Oh, no, Mama Ray, I'm the one who's sorry. You know I loved Daddy Bud like he was my own father. *(Glancing at Junior.)* And believe you me, I know what it's like to have something you love shrivel up and die right in front of you. *(Back to Raynelle.)* I just feel so bad about it.

RAYNELLE. Well, that's real sweet of you. *(Lucille re-enters with pills and water.)*

LUCILLE. Here you go, sweetheart. I brought you two.

SUZANNE. Thank you, Lucille. You're a comfort. *(She takes pills.)*

JUNIOR. Come on, Honey. Let's get you back to bed. You're gonna feel better in no time at all.

SUZANNE. I really doubt it, Junior. *(As they stand, Suzanne drops something. It hits the floor.)* Oh, my, what was that? Did I drop something?

LUCILLE. *(Retrieving it.)* Here it is. I believe you lost one of your earrings, Honey.

SUZANNE. *(Taking it.)* Oh, no, this isn't one of my earrings. I would never wear anything so cheap and tawdry looking. This must be some other woman's earring. I'll just hang onto it though. *(Straight to Junior.)* Cause I'm sure it belongs to somebody I know. And I'm sure if I think about it long enough, I'm gonna remember where I've seen it. *(Junior backs off. Lucille moves in.)*

LUCILLE. Let's get you back to bed, Sugar, before them pills kick in. *(They exit. There is a long silence. Everybody stares at Junior.)*

JUNIOR. *(Tossing a brochure on the coffee table.)* Well, my vote's in for "The Gentleman Farmer."

RAYNELLE. Well, it's awful nice. What do you think, Ray? Can we afford it?

RAY-BUD. Do you want it, Mama?

RAYNELLE. Well ... I ...

MARGUERITE. Good. Fine. It's a done deal. "Gentleman Farmer" it is. Now can we get on with the headstone before we all drop dead?

RAY-BUD.   I understand you have some thoughts on that, Aunt Marguerite.

MARGUERITE.   Yes, I do. *(Opening her Bible.)* I was thinking it'd be real nice to have some scripture on the headstone. And I've taken it upon myself to pick out a couple of things that would seem appropriate.

RAYNELLE.   Well, thank you, Marguerite.

MARGUERITE.   No trouble at all. Here's my first thought. Psalms, chapter 6, verse 5: *(She stands and reads.)*
"For in death there is no remembrance of thee
In the grave who shall give thee thanks?"
(Pause.)

ROYCE.   Well, that's cheery .

RAYNELLE.   I don't know, Marguerite. That does have kind of a sad feeling to it. You got anything else?

MARGUERITE.   Well, I'm sorry y'all didn't appreciate that. Personally, I thought it fit the bill. This here's from Ecclesiastes:
"That which hath been is now;
and that which is to be hath already been;
and God requierth that which is past."
(Pause.)

RAYNELLE.   Well, I like that a lot better.

JUNIOR.   I think we should go with it, Mama.

RAY-BUD.   Excuse me, excuse me, let's just hold on for a minute here. Mama, for the price of the stone, we get Daddy's name, date of birth, and date of departure and that's it. Anything else is extra.

JUNIOR.   How much?

RAY-BUD.   Cecil says $2.00 a letter.

JUNIOR.   Well, that wouldn't come to much.

RAY-BUD.   Whatever it comes to, it's gonna come to a damn sight more than you'll be kicking in, Junior!

JUNIOR.   What are you saying? Are you saying I'm not gonna pay my fair share? Is that what you're saying?

RAY-BUD.   Who the hell do you think is gonna pay for all this? You? Delightful? It's gonna be me, you moron!

RAYNELLE.   Now, Ray, you hush!

JUNIOR.   Well, how much is it gonna be?

RAY-BUD.   Well, I'm glad you asked me that brother. Cause I been keeping a little tally. *(Thrusts a list into his hands.)* There you go, Buddy Boy. Have a look at that. *(Junior looks over the list for a moment, mumbling a little as he does the math. When he reaches the grand total at the end of the page, he swallows hard.)*

JUNIOR.   Well, Ray, you know I'll pay you back as soon as I get back on my feet again. *(Ray-Bud punches him full in the face. They fall behind the sofa and a huge fight ensues. All the family members, including Lucille, who has just re-entered, attempt to break up the fight. Raynelle, who has not moved, quietly picks up her purse, takes out pen and paper, and writes something down. When she finishes, she begins to scream.)*

RAYNELLE.   STOP IT! STOP IT! STOP IT! STOP IT! *(The fight ends abruptly. Everyone gets to their feet. After a pause.)* Royce, honey, would you come over here please. Sit down here next to me for a minute. I want you to do me a favor. In the morning I want you to take this down to Depew's and tell Cecil this is what I want on my husband's stone. It's twelve letters and I figure this ought to cover it. *(She hands him the slip of paper and some money.)* And there's a little something in there for gas money. *(She takes his hand.)* And Royce, this is just between you and me. Do you understand?

ROYCE.   Yes, Ma'am.

RAYNELLE.   Good. Now I want to go home. *(She stands and walks out. Slowly, the others follow until Royce is left alone in the room. He pockets the money, and then tentatively opens the piece of paper.)*

ROYCE.   *(Reading.)* "Mean and Surly."

BLACKOUT

Scene 8

Later that same evening. Ray-Bud sits on his back steps, drinking from a bottle. Junior enters. He has a small Band-aid near his eye and keeps one hand behind his back.

RAY-BUD.   How's Mama?

JUNIOR.   Sleeping.

RAY-BUD.   Well, good.

JUNIOR.   I see you got yourself a little something.

RAY-BUD.   Yep. *(He takes a drink.)*

JUNIOR.   I thought you told Lucille you were gonna quit?

RAY-BUD.   Well, you know how I lie.

JUNIOR.   I won't tell her.

RAY-BUD.   That's good, Junior.

JUNIOR.   Whew-wee. Sure is hot. Hot, hot, hot. I can sure understand how a man could work up a thirst. Whew-wee. Hot.

RAY-BUD.   Sit down, Junior. *(Junior quickly sits down on the steps, producing the glass he's been hiding behind his back. Ray-Bud pours him a drink.)*

JUNIOR.   Thanks, Ray. I sure appreciate it.

RAY-BUD.   Think nothing of it. *(Pause. The both take a drink.)*

JUNIOR.   Sure is funny how things work out, isn't it?

RAY-BUD.   Yeah, I just laugh myself to sleep every night.

JUNIOR.   It's all a mystery, ain't it?

RAY-BUD.   Full of twists and turns.

JUNIOR.   We just don't know, do we?

RAY-BUD.   We're not meant to know. *(They take another drink.)*

JUNIOR.   It's okay, by the way. About my eye and all. You don't have to apologize or anything. I understand.

RAY-BUD.   Un huh.

JUNIOR.   I want you to know I was real sorry to hear about Lucille losing that last baby.

RAY-BUD.   Thank you, Junior.

JUNIOR.   Guess she was all tore up about it.

RAY-BUD.   Good God, I wish she'd just quit trying. The last time was the absolute worst. The doctor had told her if she didn't want to lose it, she was gonna have to stay flat on her back and not get up for nothing. Well, we talked about it and decided to give it one more shot. So she went to bed and I went to the Rexall to get her prescriptions filled and pick up a bedpan. And I left her this Kentucky Fried Chicken bucket in case she had to go while I was gone. Well I guess it took me about a half hour and when I got back.... Well, I don't guess I have to tell you what had happened. She'd lost it and didn't even know.

JUNIOR.   Good God, Ray. What did you do?

RAY-BUD.   Well, I called the doctor, and he told me to bring her into the office as soon as I could. God Almighty, Junior, it was a pathetic sight. Me dragging Lucille through that waiting room full of people, her screaming and crying, still holding that damn chicken bucket. *(Pause.)*

JUNIOR.   Ray, I believe that's the most awful story I ever heard. Jesus, I thought I had it bad.

RAY-BUD.   Well, I was sort of sorry to hear about your ... business going under.

JUNIOR.   Yeah, well. Thanks. Ray, did you ever wonder whether ... well, what it might have been like if you hadn't married Lucille'? I don't mean Lucille exactly. I just mean in general, do you ever wonder what your life would have been like if you had met some other woman. I don't mean a woman who can have children, cause Ray, children are not all they're cracked up to be. I just mean ... I ... do you know what I mean?

RAY-BUD.   Yeah. You mean you been screwing around on Suzanne.

JUNIOR.   How did you know?

RAY-BUD.   You been driving around in your car wearing long dangly earrings, Junior?

JUNIOR.   She tell Lucille?

RAY-BUD.   Yep.

29

JUNIOR.   Does Mama know?

RAY-BUD.   Not yet.

JUNIOR.   Oh God. I don't know, Ray. It just sort of happened. I didn't plan it or anything. I was out in the K-Mart parking lot, giving them a free cleaning, sort of as a sample, and this woman was loading some stuff into the back of her car. And she sort of struck up conversation. She asked me what I was doing. And I told her about the machine and how it worked, and she seemed real interested, you know. And Ray, I felt proud. Here I was on top of this big piece of machinery and I was sort of the master of it, you know. And here was this woman looking up at me, smiling at me. Making me feel like I was a man. A real man, like Daddy was. I was in business. I was a businessman. I had control of my life.

RAY-BUD.   Well, what happened?

JUNIOR.   Suzanne showed up! There she was looking all hot and wilted with all them kids hanging off her screaming for a popsickle. And what did she want to talk about? The car payment. The house payment. Her mother. The kids needing this and needing that. And as she was talking, I watched this woman pack up the last of her stuff, and just drive away. And all of a sudden I had this real strong desire to run Suzanne over with the machine.

RAY-BUD.   I can understand that, Junior.

JUNIOR.   But see, it got worse. As the weeks went by, and things with the business started going sour, and the bills started piling up, all I could think about was killing Suzanne. Shooting her. Pushing her down the stairs. Sneaking up on her with a baseball bat. Just anything to shut her up.

RAY-BUD.   So what happened with the woman?

JUNIOR.   One day, I just looked her up in the phone book. And one thing kinda led to another.

RAY-BUD.   How much of this does Suzanne know?

JUNIOR.   Well, I told her about the where and the when, but I kinda danced around telling her the who.

RAY-BUD.   So, what are you gonna do now?

JUNIOR.   I don't know, Ray. Everything's such a mess right now. I got to get some money.

RAY-BUD.   You will. You'll figure it out. But not tonight. *(He rises.)*

JUNIOR.   You turning in?

RAY-BUD.   Yep. Big day tomorrow. You oughta do the same.

JUNIOR.   I will in a minute.

RAY-BUD.   Junior, I was thinking maybe you could bring that thing over here, Sunday, and polish up the driveway for me. I been meaning to pay somebody to do that for me. That is, if you got the time and all.

JUNIOR.   Sure Ray, Sunday'd be good.

RAY-BUD.   Well, 'night Junior.

JUNIOR.   Ray?

RAY-BUD.   Yeah.

JUNIOR.   Daddy would sure be proud of you.

RAY-BUD.   You too, Junior. *(He exits. The lights fade on Junior, as he sits alone on the steps.)*

Scene 9

In the darkness, we hear a radio receiver searching through the frequencies until it finds a particular station. Suddenly, we hear organ music that suggests some sort of religious programming. Then the voice of the announcer.

ANNOUNCER.   Well, it's 11:45 P.M. and station WWPX, serving the communities of Lula, Timson, Tennahaw, Bobo and Blair present our nightly program of spiritual guidance and inspirational music, "Midnight Sinner," featuring the Joy of Life Singers and your host, the Reverend B.H. Hooker. *(The lights have come up during the preceding speech to reveal Reverend Hooker seated at a table, his notes and a microphone in front of him. The Joy of Life Singers, a mature quartet of singers, stand around another mike.)*

REVEREND.   Good evening, friends. This is the day that the

Lord hath made. Rejoice and be glad therein.

SINGERS. *(Uptempo, but not looking particularly joyful.)* "We've got that joy, joy, joy, joy down in our hearts. Down in our hearts. Down in our hearts. We've got that joy, joy, joy, joy down in our hearts. Down in our hearts today."

REVEREND. Real good, kids. Well, it's been a busy day and I've been in the car all day today, rushing from place to place, offering comfort and counsel to some of our brothers and sisters in crisis, catharsis and confusion. As I sat in the various kitchens, offices and hospital rooms, I was made aware of all the different kinds of problems we encounter here on this journey called life. And I said to myself, Beverly, what is this thing we call life? Is it nothing but a collection of problems, disappointments and heartache? Or do we make it that way with our endless wants, needs and desires? And if it is we ourselves who create all this unhappiness, why do we do it? Why don't we realize that the slender and fragile canoe of life can be so easily overturned in the turbulent rapids of the world? Why don't we just relax and take things as they come? And not expect so much. And why do we feel we have to call somebody when we're troubled? Why don't we just keep it to ourselves? Why do we feel the need to unload it on somebody and make them drive all the way out to our house on the hottest day of the year? Why do we cry and moan and bend somebody's ear till they think they're gonna die? Why don't we say to ourselves, before we pick up the phone, "Now is this really a problem or am I just bellyaching again?" Let us remember in these times of confusion, distress and sorrow, that when it seems you can't go on, you probably can. And when you think to yourself, there's just no answer, you're probably right. Remember friends, our time here is short. Shorter than any of us can imagine. And if you feel your life is nothing but a pit of unrelenting torture, try to make the most of it. After all, tomorrow is another day. Alright. Now we got a lot more show for you, so don't go away. We're welcoming a new sponsor to the program tonight. *(Reading from his notes.)* Depew's Funeral Home. Where they combine a thrifty, no nonsense approach with Christlike sensitivity to answer your funereal needs. Alright, kids. Take us into the commercial.

SINGERS.   "We've got that joy, joy, joy, joy down in our hearts. Down in our hearts to stay!"

BLACKOUT

END OF ACT ONE

ACT TWO

Scene 1

In the darkness, we hear a tape of a bright bouncy version of "Joy, Joy, Joy" being played on an organ. The volume is quite high. Lights come up on Marguerite standing in the middle of the community room at Depew's. A downstage center table represents the casket. She calls out to an unseen character.

MARGUERITE.   MERLINE! MERLINE! THAT'S WAY TOO LOUD! TURN IT DOWN! *(The music stops abruptly.)* This is a wake, Merline, not a parade. You got anything up there a little more somber? Well, take a look! *(Mumbling to herself.)* Paying you enough. *(As she waits, her attention turns to the casket. She pulls a handkerchief from her purse and polishes a small spot on the side of the casket. She inspects the body for a moment, then pulls out a small instamatic camera from her purse and takes a flash photograph of the casket. She glances over the body again.)* Well, Bud, they've got you painted up like a two dollar whore. *(A quieter, slower hymn comes on. It plays throughout the scene.)* What? Oh yeah, that's a lot better. And Merline, let's see if we can get that air conditioning cranked up a little. Bud's melting like a candle down here. *(Junior and Suzanne enter. Suzanne is dressed entirely in black, including a veil.)*
JUNIOR.   Well, here we are, Honey. Why don't you just sit down here for a minute. I just got to move the car. I'll be right back. Won't take but a minute. Can I get you anything, Sweetheart?
SUZANNE.   *(Pulling back her veil.)* Can you get me back the last twelve years of my life, Junior? Can you get me back my youth, my hopes, my dreams of a good life with a loving and faithful husband? Can you do that, Junior?
JUNIOR.   No, but I could get you a Coke or something.
SUZANNE.   A Coke would be fine, adulterer.

JUNIOR. Aw, Suzanne ... *(A huge crash is heard offstage. Junior runs to the door.)* YOU KIDS GET OUT OF HERE! I TOLD Y'ALL TO WAIT IN THE CAR! I'll be right back, Baby. *(A yelping sound is heard offstage.)* AND GET THEM DOGS OUT OF HERE! *(He exits.)*

MARGUERITE. Suzanne.

SUZANNE. *(Fixing her make-up.)* Aunt Marguerite.

MARGUERITE. You feeling better today?

SUZANNE. Yes, thank you.

MARGUERITE. Well, I hope you'll feel up to singing tomorrow morning.

SUZANNE. *(Crossing up to her.)* Oh, of course I will. I just couldn't let Daddy Bud down. Aw, doesn't he look wonderful. So peaceful.

MARGUERITE. Looks kinda rouged up to me.

SUZANNE. How's she gonna go on, Aunt Marguerite? That's what I'd like to know. How's she gonna go on?

MARGUERITE. Well, it's gonna be sad.

SUZANNE. How's she gonna face life without our Daddy Bud?

MARGUERITE. It's sad when a woman loses her husband. I remember when I lost my William. No one to cook for. No one to keep house for. Nobody to talk to over the breakfast table. The children crying. Asking over and over again for their daddy. "Where's my Daddy?" Nothing but the lonesome sound of the boards creaking under your feet as you walk the floor from dark to dawn asking yourself that same question: Why — Oh Why — Oh Why — Oh? *(Suzanne is weeping openly.)* Why did he leave me? Where has he gone? Why don't he come back? Why can't it all be the way it was? No, I don't think there's anything sadder than a woman losing her man. *(Suzanne explodes into tears and throws herself across the casket, sobbing deeply. Disgusted, Marguerite pulls Suzanne off the casket.)* Suzanne, get a hold of yourself! *(Polishing a spot on the casket again.)* You know for what we're paying, it wouldn't have killed Merline to run a little Pledge across this thing. *(Ray-Bud, Raynelle, Lucille, and Delightful, who is chewing bubble gum, enter. They stand quietly in the doorway for a moment.)*

35

RAY-BUD.   Well, here we are. You want to sit down for a minute?

RAYNELLE.   No, let's have a look at him. *(They move slowly up to the casket and survey the body.)*

LUCILLE.   Well, doesn't he look nice. You were so right about that blue suit. Makes him look so distinguished.

RAYNELLE.   Yes, it does.

LUCILLE.   I think Cecil did a wonderful job. He looks just like he's sleeping, doesn't he, Ray?

RAY-BUD.   *(Horrified.)* Yeah.

MARGUERITE.   Looks kinda like "Miss Kitty" on *Gunsmoke* to me.

LUCILLE.   Oh, I don't think so. I think he looks real natural. Don't you, Suzanne? *(Suzanne explodes into tears again. Everyone stares at her for a moment.)* Well, what do you think, Delightful? *(Delightful, who is blowing a huge bubble, shrugs her shoulders, then crosses and sits in the chair previously occupied by Suzanne.)*

RAYNELLE.   It's fine. He looks fine.

RAY-BUD.   What has he got on his feet?

LUCILLE.   Oh yeah, Ray, I forgot to tell you. Cecil called this afternoon and said they had a little problem with the shoes we sent over.

RAY-BUD.   Those were brand new shoes.

LUCILLE.   Yes, I know, Ray. You remember how Daddy Bud always had that arthritis in his feet so bad? Well, they think that when he had his stroke, he sort of pointed his toes down and well ... they sorta stayed that way. So there was just no way to get him in those shoes, and it was so late and all. So they just did the best they could.

RAY-BUD.   Lucille, my Daddy's wearing ballet shoes. *(Pause.)*

LUCILLE.   Well, I think they make him look real graceful.

RAY-BUD.   I'm gonna kill Cecil.

LUCILLE.   Ray, we got people coming! We can't have him out here in his stocking feet. How would that look?

RAYNELLE.   It's fine, Ray. We can bring his bedroom slippers tomorrow.

RAY-BUD.   I'm gonna kill him.

36

MARGUERITE. I'll tell you who I'm gonna kill. Merline, if she don't get that air conditioning turned up. *(As she exits.)* Merline! Where are you? Bud's getting awful shiny out here!

LUCILLE. Well, I guess I oughta find Cecil and see about getting those food tables set up. *(Delicately.)* Suzanne, Honey, would you like to come with me? *(Suzanne, unable to speak, nods her head.)* Come on, Sugar. Maybe you oughta freshen up a little. You've just about cried all your Mabeline off. *(They exit with Suzanne bawling at the top of her lungs.)*

RAYNELLE. I had no idea Suzanne was so close to Bud.

RAY-BUD. Mama, can I get you anything? Would you like to sit down or something?

RAYNELLE. No, Ray. I'm fine. I just want to stand here for a minute. You go ahead if you want to.

RAY-BUD. No, that's alright. We'll just stand here for a minute. That's what we'll do. We'll just stand right here. *(Wiping his forehead.)* Whew! Sure is warm in here, ain't it? I sure hope Marguerite can get the air conditioning turned up. Whew! It's warm.

RAYNELLE. Are you alright, Ray?

RAY-BUD. Oh yeah, Mama. I'm fine. *(Junior comes running in carrying a Coke.)*

JUNIOR. I'm sorry, Honey! Mayfield's was closed and I couldn't find a place to park and ... *(He finds Delightful sitting where Suzanne had been. Approaching the others.)* Y'all seen Suzanne?

RAY-BUD. Lucille took her to the toilet. I think they're gonna be in there for a while.

JUNIOR. Well, shoot! I ran all the way down to.... Aw shoot! Here. *(He hands the Coke to Delightful, who has been eyeing it since his entrance. He notices the body for the first time.)* Wow! Would you look at that. *(He leans in for a better look.)* I mean he looks dead, doesn't he, Ray?

RAY-BUD. You expect him to be singing and dancing, Junior?

JUNIOR. No, but I didn't expect him to look so damn dead.

RAYNELLE. Come on, Delightful. Let's hit the ladies room

before everybody gets here. It's gonna be a long sit. *(Raynelle and Delightful exit. The brothers look at the body.)*

JUNIOR.   Well, there it is, Ray. Death. Mortality. The Grim Reaper staring ya right in the face.

RAY-BUD.   *(Truly sick.)* Shut up, Junior.

JUNIOR.   What's the matter, Ray?

RAY-BUD.   Nothin'.

JUNIOR.   You don't look too good, Ray.

RAY-BUD.   I can't move, Junior.

JUNIOR.   What do you mean you can't move?

RAY-BUD.   Get me out of here, Junior. I need some air.

JUNIOR.   *(As he slowly helps him out.)* It's nothing to be scared of, Ray. It's just death. The end of the line. The last hurrah. Crossing the River Jordan.

RAY-BUD.   Shut up, Junior.

JUNIOR.   Why does Daddy have them dancing shoes on?

RAY-BUD.   I'll tell you later. Listen, Junior, when I'm feeling a little better, I want you to help me do something.

JUNIOR.   Sure, Ray. What are we gonna do?

RAY-BUD.   *(As they are exiting.)* We're gonna beat the shit out of Cecil Depew.

BLACKOUT

Scene 2

The visitation takes place in the various corners of the community room at Depew's. The lights come up on Raynelle, who is seated with Veda and Norval, an elderly couple.

VEDA.   Well, we sure were sorry to hear about Bud.

RAYNELLE.   Thank you, Veda. Norval's looking better than he did the last time I saw him.

VEDA.   Well, he has his good days and his bad days. AIN'T THAT RIGHT, NORVAL? *(Norval mumbles something unintelligible.)*

RAYNELLE.   What did he say?

VEDA.   I believe he said: "The corn eats many miles." *(She pats his hand.)* THAT'S GOOD, NORVAL!

RAYNELLE.   THAT'S REAL GOOD, NORVAL!

VEDA.   Every once in a while, Norval takes a little walk through the garden, if you know what I mean.

RAYNELLE.   Well. How are you doing, Veda? Haven't seen you in so long.

VEDA.   Oh, not so bad, I guess. I still manage to get out to services on Sunday. And of course, we go into Timson every Wednesday for Norval's dialysis and to get his prescriptions filled. The doctor's got him on these new liver pills that seem to be working out a lot better. AIN'T THAT RIGHT, NORVAL? *(Norval seems to have fallen asleep.)* NORVAL! *(She pokes him.)* NORVAL! *(He stirs and mumbles something else.)* Whew. I thought we'd lost him for a minute there. I got to remember to get them batteries changed on his pacemaker. Since he had his bypass done and his gallbladder out, I've noticed a real improvement. *(She takes a small pill box out of her purse and shakes it. Responding to the sound, Norval opens his mouth and tilts his head back. Veda begins to feed pills to Norval as she talks.)* AND NEXT MONTH, WE'RE GETTING RID OF THAT PROSTATE AREN'T WE, NORVAL? Of course, we got to keep that blood pressure down, and this one's for his stomach, and this one keeps them kidneys working. I'll tell you, it's a lot to remember. *(She takes the last pill herself.)*

RAYNELLE.   I can imagine. *(Veda takes a small tank of oxygen out of her bag and hands Norval the mask, which he places over his nose and mouth.)*

VEDA.   *(As she turns the valve.)* Of course, Verna Swindell comes in twice a week to help me with his bath and all. And she sits with him if I have to go into town. YA GETTING ANYTHING NORVAL? Of course, he's on a real strict diet so I got to be real careful what he eats. No salt, no sugar, no fat, no meat, no dairy, nothing too spicy, nothing too heavy. *(Pulling a small package out of her bag.)* YOU WANT A CRACKER? *(He shakes his head.)* Cracker, Ray?

RAYNELLE.   *(Taking one.)* Thank you, Veda.

39

VEDA. *(Taking one herself.)* Yeah, after we get his physical therapy out of the way in the morning, I give him his injections and irrigate him for about an hour. Once he's had his lunch, he takes a good long nap, and then I usually put him out on the porch and let him watch the sun set while I get supper ready. I got to be careful though. One time I got to talking on the phone and left him out there for over an hour, and the mosquitos got him pretty bad. Of course, supper's his big meal of the day, so it's always a gamble to see if he's gonna be able to keep it down. Once I get his evening medication done and get him into bed, he usually sleeps through till morning. Of course, I don't get too much sleep myself since I have to get up and turn him every couple of hours. *(Pause.)*

RAYNELLE. Well, you're just so lucky to have him.

VEDA. I know. *(Norval mumbles something.)* WHAT'D YOU SAY? *(He repeats it.)* UH HUH! OKAY!

RAYNELLE. What was it?

VEDA. I'm not exactly sure. Sounded like something about Debbie Reynolds. *(Pause.)*

RAYNELLE. *(Overlapping.)* WELL, THAT'S GOOD, NORVAL! THAT'S REAL GOOD!

VEDA. *(Overlapping.)* THAT'S GOOD! THAT'S REAL GOOD, NORVAL!

BLACKOUT

Scene 3

Lucille sits with Nadine, a young woman. They look at a long string of photographs from Nadine's wallet. She is holding a baby and is hugely pregnant with another.

NADINE. This one's Perry Como. He's by my first marriage to A.C. You remember him?

LUCILLE. Oh sure.

NADINE. And this is Alan Alda and that's Linda Evans there

40

in the back. *(Pointing off.)* And that one over there is Charles Bronson. And then there's the twins, Ann-Margret and Anne Murray. *(Referring to the baby in her arms.)* And this here's Farrah-Zsa Zsa.

LUCILLE. Aw, isn't she beautiful. They're all just so precious, Nadine.

NADINE. Thank you, Lucille.

LUCILLE. And you named them all after someone famous.

NADINE. Yes, I did. Call me a fool, but I've always thought each of 'em was special in some way. And I just figured if you're special, you should have a special name. Excuse me, Lucille. *(Calling off.)* OPRAH, PUT THAT DOWN! PUT IT DOWN!

LUCILLE. Well, honey you're just so lucky to have all these precious babies. Ray-Bud and I have tried so many times but I just never seem to be able to carry to term.

NADINE. Oh, I just know it'll all work out for you. You would be such a good mother and I know how happy Ray-Bud would be.

LUCILLE. Oh he would. You know he never talks about it, but I just know how bad he wants one.

NADINE. Well, eighth time's a charm that's what I've always heard.

LUCILLE. Nadine, can you keep a secret?

NADINE. Oh, sure.

LUCILLE. Now, this is a surprise, so don't breathe a word of it, cause I don't want to get everybody's hopes up ... but ... well ...

NADINE. Lucille, you're not!

LUCILLE. "My friend" is almost a week late.

NADINE. Oh, Lucille, that's just wonderful!

LUCILLE. Well, it's just a week, but I've got my fingers crossed.

NADINE. Oh mine too. That would just be so wonderful. Y'all have been together so long.

LUCILLE. Almost fifteen years.

NADINE. Fifteen years. You know it's just so funny how things work out. Here you and Ray-Bud been together so long and wanting children so bad. To tell you the truth, Lucille, I never really planned on having a big family.

LUCILLE.   Really?

NADINE.   No, I sorta had this plan to move out to Hollywood, but then I met A.C., and then I met Carl ... and then I met Wendell and then I met Duane. And things just sorta didn't work out.

LUCILLE.   Well, Honey, you're young. You could still go out there.

NADINE.   No. After Geraldo was born, I pretty much gave up on that idea. But the good news is I'm engaged again.

LUCILLE.   Oh good for you, Honey.

NADINE.   It's love this time, Lucille. He's nothing like those other men. I got a real good feeling about it.

LUCILLE.   Oh how wonderful! Well, tell me all about him!

NADINE.   Well, his name is Rebel, and he works for the carnival. Travels all over the country guessing people's weight. The only problem is he doesn't like kids. I'm not gonna worry about it though.

LUCILLE.   Love conquers all.

NADINE.   It sure does.

LUCILLE.   A person's just got to follow their heart.

NADINE.   Amen.

LUCILLE.   You just got to do what you feel's best.

NADINE.   Call me a fool.

LUCILLE.   You're a fool.

BLACKOUT

Scene 4

Ray-Bud and Clyde, his boss. Clyde wears his blue garage uniform and drinks a can of beer as he speaks.

CLYDE.   Well shit, Ray. It's all a mystery ain't it. Life. Death.

RAY-BUD.   Yes, it is.

42

CLYDE. We just don't know, do we?

RAY-BUD. No, we don't.

CLYDE. We're not meant to know.

RAY-BUD. No, we're not.

CLYDE. Least it was quick.

RAY-BUD. Yes, it was.

CLYDE. That's the best way, you know. Quick. You don't want to linger. That's awful.

RAY-BUD. Yeah, it is.

CLYDE. Quick. That's how I want to go. Bolt of lightning. Car crash. Piano falling on my head. That's what I want.

RAY-BUD. Well, I hope that happens to you, Clyde.

CLYDE. Me too, Ray. Wouldn't want to just hang on and hang on. That's no good.

RAY-BUD. No.

CLYDE. Wouldn't want to be in a coma either.

RAY-BUD. Nope.

CLYDE. You see the flowers me and the boys sent over?

RAY-BUD. Oh yeah, I did. Thank you, Clyde. That was real thoughtful.

CLYDE. "Clyde's Auto Repair and Body Shop" take care of their own, Ray.

RAY-BUD. Well, I sure appreciate it.

CLYDE. We're not just a garage, Ray. We're a family. When you were nothing but a drunken bum and didn't show up for work half the time, we stood by you, 'cause that's what families do. They look out for each other. You just let me know if you have any problems around here. We'll take care of 'em. *(He winks at him.)*

RAY-BUD. What are you talking about?

CLYDE. You say the word and they'll be paying out more in hearse repair than they can make in a year.

RAY-BUD. Thank you, Clyde.

CLYDE. We take care of our own, Ray.

RAY-BUD. I know you do.

CLYDE. They park that thing right out on the street, you know. Anything in the world could happen to it, if you get my meaning. You say the word and that thing might just blow up some night.

RAY-BUD.   I'll keep that in mind.

CLYDE.   Stranger things have happened, Ray. My brother-in-law's in the demolition business, you know.

RAY-BUD.   I got the picture, Clyde.

CLYDE.   You just let me know.

RAY-BUD.   I will.

CLYDE.   It's times like these you find out who your real friends are. You find out all sorts of strange and mysterious things. Speaking of which ... you never told me your Daddy was a dancer, Ray. *(Pause.)*

RAY-BUD.   Well, that's a pretty well kept secret.

BLACKOUT

Scene 5

Junior stands outside the bathroom door. Two chairs sit next to the door.

JUNIOR.   Honey? Baby? People are asking about you. You're not gonna stay in there all night are you? 'Cause I really need you out here. Honey, I know what you're thinking. But I didn't do what you're thinking I did. Well, I mean, I did it. I definitely did it. I just didn't do it for the reasons you're thinking I did it. I did it ... I did it ... *(He pulls a chair up next to the door and sits.)* Whew! You know maybe I could just start over here for a minute. Baby, do you remember what it was like when we first started dating? How happy we were? How much fun we had? But you know what I remember most about that time? It was when I we used to stop by the Dairy Queen and I'd buy you a grape slush. And then I'd take you home and we'd sit out on that sofa your folks had out in their front yard. And we'd just talk about the future and how it was gonna be. I miss that, Honey. I miss who I was then. And I miss who you were then too. And I guess standing out there in that parking lot I sorta lost my head, and I just forgot how much you and the kids mean to me. And I'm hoping you can find it in your heart to forgive me. 'Cause you're my whole world and I love you. *(The bathroom door opens and Royce comes out wiping his hands on a paper towel.)*

ROYCE. Thanks, Junior. I love you too.

JUNIOR. Royce, you haven't seen Suzanne, have you?

ROYCE. Yeah, I think she's helping Lucille out in the kitchen.

JUNIOR. Okay. Well, thanks.

ROYCE. Things aren't going too well, are they Junior?

JUNIOR. Well, that's one way of putting it. Listen, Royce, I got some pretty complicated things to think over here, so if you don't mind ... *(Junior wanders over and sits in one of the chairs.)*

ROYCE. Answers are sure hard to come by, aren't they, Junior?

JUNIOR. Yeah, they are.

ROYCE. Sometimes a man's just got to sit down and think it all through doesn't he. *(Royce plops down in the chair beside Junior.)*

JUNIOR. Yep.

ROYCE. Well, Junior, this is how I see it. Life is like a big circle. And you don't know where it began and you just never know how it's all gonna end. That's the way I see it.

JUNIOR. So, life is a circle.

ROYCE. Yeah. But the trouble is all some people see is the circle itself. And they feel trapped inside it. Like they'll never get out. And before too long, all they can think about is all the things they wish they had inside their circle. Jim-Ed was always one of those kind of people. So much so that when that highway patrolman pulled him over, he had quite a few things in the trunk of his car that actually belonged in some other people's circles. So for the next three to five years, Jim-Ed's circle is gonna be about eight feet by eight feet.

JUNIOR. How's he liking it since they transferred him up to Parkersville?

ROYCE. Oh, he likes it okay, I guess.

JUNIOR. Making a lot of new friends, is he?

ROYCE. Well, it's hard you know, when you move to a new place.

JUNIOR. Well, sure.

ROYCE. You see, Junior, what Jim-Ed didn't understand was the circle ain't something that's outside you. It's something that's inside you. It doesn't keep you from having things, it just protects what you already got. And the funny thing is that when you stop pushing and punching and trying to get out of it ... when you finally just let go, the circle sorta opens up a little. And all of sudden, you got room for everything. Room for Jim-Ed. Room for Mama. Room for all the things that didn't quite work out. And just a little bit left over for all the things that might just work out yet. You know what I mean, Junior?

JUNIOR. So, what you're saying is ... life is a circle.

ROYCE. Well, yeah. You know, I guess we better be getting in there. Food's gonna be out in a minute.

JUNIOR. Royce, if you don't mind my asking. How did you happen to figure out that life is a circle.

ROYCE. Well, Junior. In the sewage business, you tend to let your mind roam a lot. Cause if you ever thought about what you're actually doing, I believe you'd snap.

BLACKOUT

Scene 6

Lucille, Suzanne, Delightful and Juanita, an attractive and expensively dressed woman enter. Each carries a covered dish. Throughout the scene, the food table is gradually set up with a table cloth, Tupperware, paper plates, etc. After Suzanne deposits her dish on the table, she crosses over, sits, takes off one of her shoes and rubs her foot.

JUANITA. Well, I can't believe how many old friends I've seen here tonight. People I haven't seen since high school.

I'm just so sorry Teddy-Wayne couldn't be here. He always loved his uncle Bud so much. But his law practice is just doing so well it just keeps him busy day and night. Why I just feel like I hardly ever see him.

LUCILLE.   Aw, that's such a shame.

JUANITA.   Suzanne, Honey, since you're not doing anything, would you mind to give us a hand with this. *(Suzanne replaces her shoe and crosses back to the table. She seems to be at a bit of a loss as to what exactly she's supposed to be doing. As soon as Suzanne vacates her chair, Delightful pulls it up next to the table, sits, and begins to eat a package of M&Ms she has brought with her.)* I'll tell you what's a shame. It's a shame it takes something this sad to bring us all together again. Suzanne, do you remember how Lucille was a part of my royal court when I was elected Yam Queen.

SUZANNE.   Seems to me I remember that.

JUANITA.   *(Placing her arm around Lucille.)* Oh, that was just such a wonderful time. All of us up on that beautiful float. Why, I can still remember the faces of all those other girls just floating by like so much garbage. Why, I believe we were just the prettiest girls in this town.

LUCILLE.   *(Glancing at Suzanne.)* Oh, I don't know about that! Well, I mean, you were certainly pretty. Why, I believe you were just about the prettiest Yam Queen we ever had. Don't you think so, Suzanne?

SUZANNE.   *(Plopping a dish down on the table.)* Well, about as pretty as a woman can be with a big pile of yams sitting on her head.

LUCILLE.   Oh, that was all such a long time ago. It's just so good to know that we're all a family now. And we can come together like this in a time of sadness.

JUANITA.   You are so right, Lucille. You can't be living in the past. It's so important at a time like this to be kind and loving to each other. So, how are things with you, Suzanne?

SUZANNE.   Well, Juanita, I feel like my life has come to an end. Like everything I ever dreamed of has died a slow and horrible death. And that my whole world was built on sand.

JUANITA.   Oh Honey, I'm so sorry to hear that. Well, chin

up! Lucille, did you see what happened to my peach cobbler?

LUCILLE.   Oh Honey, it must still be out in the kitchen.

JUANITA.   Oh don't worry, Sugar. I'll get it. Delightful, you want to help us in here for a minute. And Lucille, you might want to put some of those covers back on. I'm sure Merline's got roaches. This place is such a sty. *(Juanita and Delightful exit. Suzanne and Lucille look at each other.)*

SUZANNE.   She's gonna be Yam Queen till the day she dies.

LUCILLE.   Oh, don't pay any attention to her, Honey. She just thinks she's happy.

SUZANNE.   Oh Lucille, what am I gonna do? What am I gonna do? *(Suzanne crosses back to her chair and sits.)*

LUCILLE.   Oh, Honey, it'll be alright. Things aren't so bad. No matter what happens you got three beautiful, healthy children. And ... ah.... You got your job there at Newberry's, and you got a mobile home, and you ... you got a ... you got a ...

SUZANNE.   Go on, say it, Lucille. I got a parking lot machine! *(Suzanne bursts into tears, just as Marguerite and Juanita enter carrying more covered dishes. Marguerite glances at Suzanne as they enter.)*

MARGUERITE.   Well, it's good to know some things never change. We got a lot more food out there in the kitchen!

LUCILLE.   Come on, Honey. Why don't you give me a hand in the kitchen for a minute. *(Lucille and Suzanne exit.)*

JUANITA.   Well, Aunt Marguerite, are you still working with your church groups and all?

MARGUERITE.   Yes, I am. I'm currently vice president and sergeant-at-arms for the Ladies African Missionary Auxiliary.

JUANITA.   Oh, I been reading so much about that sort of thing. Y'all gonna teach them to grow their own food and all.

MARGUERITE.   No, we feel that's been done to death. When them lazy savages get hungry enough, they'll figure out how to put a seed in the ground. No, we're sponsoring the ministry of Sister Wylene Erger, who's gonna go over there and teach them African women how to wear brassieres.

JUANITA.   Well. How's that going?

MARGUERITE.   Well, we don't have all the money raised yet, but we're gonna get them women in brassieres if it's the last thing we do.

JUANITA.   Well, I sure wish you luck with that. *(Lucille, Suzanne and Delightful re-enter. They bring with them the last of the covered dishes and a large brown paper sack. After placing her dish on the corner of the table closest to her, Delightful resumes her seat.)*

LUCILLE.   Well, I think this is the last of it. Aw, doesn't everything look nice. Well, I guess we ought to get some of these people fed. *(The women line up behind the serving table in the following order: Juanita, Lucille, Marguerite and Suzanne.)*

JUANITA.   Oh look, Lucille, isn't that Bernice Talbot leaving?

LUCILLE.   Yes, I believe it is.

JUANITA.   God, she looks awful. Not that she ever was a prize.

LUCILLE.   Well, she always had that skin problem.

MARGUERITE.   Of course you know she drinks.

SUZANNE.   And her mother went insane.

JUANITA.   And she never could dress.

LUCILLE.   Why does she wear that awful jewelry?

MARGUERITE.   And all that make-up.

SUZANNE.   She'd throw up her skirt for anybody who'd ask.

JUANITA.   It's a shame.

LUCILLE.   Poor thing.

MARGUERITE.   Bless her heart.

SUZANNE.   God love her.

LUCILLE.   Well, I guess we better get started.

JUANITA.   Of course, you know she picks up men in the K-Mart parking lot.

LUCILLE.   *(Speaking out front, somewhat nervous about being in the spotlight.)* Well, I noticed some of you all have been a little bit shy about coming up to the food table. I know nobody wants to be first, but we got some awful good things up here. What's that you have there, Juanita?

JUANITA.   *(Totally in her element, reading from the attached card.)* This comes to us from Oveda and Cleatus Biddick. Oveda sends their condolences and says she discovered this recipe one day when a page of her cookbook fell out and she accidently made half of one dish and half of another. She calls it "Macaroni and Ham Loaf Surprise with Cheese" and it sure looks good.

LUCILLE.   It sure does! Uh.... What's that you have down there, Delightful?

DELIGHTFUL.   *(Examining it without leaving her chair.)* Beans. *(Slight pause.)*

LUCILLE.   Well, alright. Delightful's got beans if anybody wants 'em. Aunt Marguerite?

MARGUERITE.   Well, Suzanne brought this bag of potato chips. Of course, she didn't bring a bowl or anything, so I guess she just expects you all to just stick your hand down in this bag.

LUCILLE.   Suzanne, Honey, what have you got down there that the folks might like to know about?

SUZANNE.   Well, we got some kinda ... *(The penny drops.)* Bernice Talbot picks up men in the K-Mart parking lot?

LUCILLE.   *(Quickly picking something up.)* Next, we have a real nice ...

SUZANNE.   BERNICE TALBOT PICKS UP MEN IN THE K-MART PARKING LOT?

LUCILLE.   Suzanne, Honey, maybe we could talk about that a little bit ...

JUANITA.   Suzanne!

SUZANNE.   MY HUSBAND DID IT WITH THAT DOG IN THE K-MART PARKING LOT! I CAN'T STAND IT! *(Suzanne wales and collapses behind the food table. There is a short stunned silence.)*

MARGUERITE.   *(To Lucille and Juanita.)* Don't pay her any mind. She just wants attention. Alright, Lucille, what else is left?

SUZANNE.   *(A disembodied voice.)* Bernice Talbot!

MARGUERITE.   Would you quit harping on that! Now get up before you get your dress dirty! *(Suzanne slowly gets to her feet.)*

LUCILLE.   Well, this doesn't have a card with it but it looks like somebody brought us some ... *(Lucille pulls from the brown paper sack, a large bucket of Kentucky Fried Chicken. She is frozen for a moment, then tries to recover.)* Some.... Some real tasty ...

WHO BROUGHT THIS! *(Lucille bursts into tears and goes running from the room. Juanita follows.)*
JUANITA. *(As she exits.)* Lucille! Honey! What's the matter? *(Suzanne attempts to run after them and gets as far as the doorway.)*
SUZANNE. Lucille! Come back! Who's gonna do this?
MARGUERITE. Suzanne! I just got one question. Are we gonna serve this meal or are we all gonna sit in the toilet and cry all night? *(Suzanne slowly makes her way back to the table.)* Well, alright then. Now stand up straight and have a little pride for once in your life. I've got a son in the penitentiary and you don't see me wallering on the floor. These people don't care what your husband did with Bernice Talbot. They never liked you before, you think they're gonna think less of you now? So, let's get this done. *(Marguerite shoots a look over at Delightful, who rises and takes a place at the food table. Marguerite, Suzanne and Delightful each pick up a dish. Marguerite speaks out front.)* Alright, now who wants the ham loaf?

BLACKOUT

Scene 7

Raynelle and Lucille in Raynelle's bedroom. Later that night. Lucille is folding some clothing. Raynelle is wiping off Bud's slippers.

LUCILLE. Well, we sure had a nice turn out tonight.
RAYNELLE. Yes, we did.
LUCILLE. I'm sorry I got so sick. I just don't know what came over me. I sure hated not being able to see everybody.
RAYNELLE. Trust me, Lucille. You didn't miss that much.
LUCILLE. I just thought it was so sweet. All those people. Each one of them touched in some way by Daddy Bud.
RAYNELLE. Yeah, they're all touched alright. Lucille, hand me that bag. *(She places slippers inside.)*
LUCILLE. It's funny what will bring people together. All

51

gathered together in one place like that.

RAYNELLE. I think it might have had something to do with the free meal they just got.

LUCILLE. Oh, now you don't mean that.

RAYNELLE. No, I don't guess I do. People mean well. They come there wanting to tell you how sorry they are for you and they wind up telling you how sorry they are for themselves, and by the end of the evening, you sort of feel like slitting your throat.

LUCILLE. Oh, you're just tired, Mama Ray.

RAYNELLE. *(Handing her the bag.)* Set this down by the door so we don't forget it tomorrow. And would you see if Junior can use any of them shirts. If he's gonna be job hunting, we can't have him going out looking like a scarecrow.

LUCILLE. I will. *(Ray-Bud enters.)* You about ready to go, Honey?

RAY-BUD. No, I got to talk to Mama for a little while. You don't mind do you, Lucille?

LUCILLE. Not a bit. *(To Raynelle.)* You get some sleep.

RAYNELLE. 'Night Honey. *(Lucille exits.)* Ray.

RAY-BUD. Mama.

RAYNELLE. You know, Ray, it's funny how you can feel like you know somebody and then you find out something about them you never knew. That ever happen to you, Ray?

RAY-BUD. Yeah, I guess it has.

RAYNELLE. Take your Daddy for instance. Here I was married to him for almost forty years and he never once said a word to me about defecting from that Russian ballet company. You wouldn't happen to know anything about that, would you?

RAY-BUD. I'm sorry, Mama. I don't know why I said that. Something just came over me. I didn't mean to embarrass you.

RAYNELLE. You should have some respect, Ray.

RAY-BUD. Yeah, well it's funny you should mention that, Mama, 'cause that's exactly what brings me here tonight. Cecil told me what you had requested on the stone. I'm not having it, Mama. He may have been your husband, and I know you all had your problems, but he was my father, and I'm not

52

having it. It's gonna say "Rest in Peace" which is only eleven letters, so Cecil's gonna give us a two dollar credit.

RAYNELLE.   I understand, Ray. It's alright. *(She reaches down and picks up her purse.)*

RAY-BUD.   Well, that's all I had to say. I'll let you get to sleep now.

RAYNELLE.   Sit down for a minute. I want to show you something. *(She pulls a pair of scissors from her purse.)* Do you remember these?

RAY-BUD.   No.

RAYNELLE.   There's no reason you should. You were just a little boy. These are my old sewing scissors. My mother gave them to me not long after Bud and I were married. Lord knows all the things I made with these. Quilts for the beds. Clothes for you boys. And then one day, they just disappeared. Searched this house from top to bottom and never could find them. They were just lost. And they stayed lost for twenty-seven years. I can't tell you the number of times I wondered whatever happened to these things. And do you know where I found them?

RAY-BUD.   No.

RAYNELLE.   In your Daddy's shoebox yesterday. Ain't that funny? Reckon how many thousands of times I must have walked right past them, never knowing they were in there. I can't imagine what he wanted with them. But the real funny thing is in all them twenty-seven years, it never once occurred to me to ask Bud if he knew where they were. Ain't that strange?

RAY-BUD.   Yeah, I guess it is.

RAYNELLE.   I didn't lose your Daddy, Wednesday morning, Ray. I lost him a long, long time ago. But you know what? I think he'll turn up one of these days. And it'll be just like finding these scissors. Maybe I'll be opening a drawer or cleaning out a closet, and there he'll be. Well, I don't mean "him" exactly. I don't expect he'll be flying through the house in a white sheet or anything. Just a feeling. Like I had when I found these things. Not real happy and not real sad. Just glad, I guess. Glad it all happened. Glad I knew him. *(Pause.)* Well, do you think your old Mama has lost her mind.

RAY-BUD.   No, I don't.

RAYNELLE.   Well, you're wrong. I have.

RAY-BUD.   So, what are you gonna do with your new-found sewing scissors?

RAYNELLE.   Well, after Junior goes through 'em, I'm gonna cut up all your Daddy's clothes and make me a real pretty quilt.

RAY-BUD.   Sounds like a good idea. Well, it's late. We better get to bed. *(He stands and starts out.)*

RAYNELLE.   Don't let me forget those slippers in the morning. It would be just like me to remember those things after they've already thrown the dirt in.

RAY-BUD.   *(At the door.)* I'll remember. 'Night Mama.

RAYNELLE.   Ray.

RAY-BUD.   Yeah.

RAYNELLE.   You just got to be patient, Honey. He'll come back to you too. Just when you least expect it.

RAY-BUD.   See you in the morning. *(He exits.)*

RAYNELLE.   *(Opening and closing the scissors.)* Well, Bud, you remember that pretty plaid shirt I gave you last Christmas and you never wore? Well, it's mine now.

BLACKOUT

Scene 8

In the darkness, we hear a rush of somewhat melodramatic organ music. After a flourish, the music calms down to a slow dirge which continues as the lights come up on the funeral scene.

There are four rows of chairs, two on each side of a center aisle. Ray-Bud, Raynelle and Delightful are seated together in one of the front rows. Behind them are Marguerite and Royce. Across the aisle, in the second row, Suzanne is seated by herself. The organ music drones on. Marguerite rises and begins to pace up the aisle.

MARGUERITE. I can't believe how long this is taking.

ROYCE. Just relax, Mama.

MARGUERITE. "And the mother of Sisera looked out a window, and cried through the lattice, Why is his chariot so long in coming? *(Somewhat for Ray-Bud's benefit.)* Why tarry the wheels of the chariot?"

ROYCE. Mama, why don't you just park your chariot here for a minute. *(Marguerite resumes her seat.)*

RAY-BUD. Where the hell is he?

RAYNELLE. We're in no rush, Ray. He probably had to make a call.

RAY-BUD. We're paying by the hour, Mama.

RAYNELLE. Go find him.

RAY-BUD. Sit tight. *(Ray-Bud makes his way up the aisle, when he runs into Juanita entering. She seems very distressed.)* Hello, Juanita.

JUANITA. Oh Ray, I'm sorry I'm so late. I sorta got held up at the beauty shop.

RAY-BUD. You didn't miss anything, Juanita. We can't seem to find the preacher. I'm real glad you could come. *(He starts to exit, she pulls him aside.)*

JUANITA. Ray, does my hair look alright?

RAY-BUD. Yeah, Juanita, it looks fine.

JUANITA. Really? My regular girl was out sick, and Retha Middleton had to do it. And you know she's none too dependable since she had that accident. How she picks up those hot rollers with her teeth is a mystery to me.

RAY-BUD. Maybe you better find a seat, Juanita. We're gonna be starting in a minute here.

JUANITA. Thank you, Ray. I will. *(Juanita hurries down the aisle and sits beside Suzanne. Ray-Bud has just reached the doorway when Lucille appears.)*

RAY-BUD. There you are! Where the hell is he?

LUCILLE. He'll be out in a minute, Ray.

RAY-BUD. I'm going broke waiting for him. We were supposed to start this thing at eleven. What's the hold up back there?

LUCILLE.   Did you know that last night was the Reverend and Mrs. Hooker's anniversary?

RAY-BUD.   No, I didn't.

LUCILLE.   Neither did I and I just feel so bad we didn't send 'em a card!

RAY-BUD.   What's the point, Lucille?

LUCILLE.   Well, they decided since it was a special occasion and all, they decided they'd try out that new Mexican restaurant up in Timson.

RAY-BUD.   So?

LUCILLE.   Well, he's having a little ... intestinal difficulty this morning. *(Pause.)*

RAY-BUD.   You have got to be kidding me?

LUCILLE.   Do I look like I'm kidding?

RAY-BUD.   Go knock on that door and tell him to get out here!

LUCILLE.   Ray! I can't do that! He's the preacher! I'd die of shame!

RAY-BUD.   If I have to come in there myself, I'm gonna tear it off the hinges! I've just about had it with this shit!

LUCILLE.   Well, that was a poor choice of words!

RAY-BUD.   Just do it, Lucille!

LUCILLE.   Alright! But I know I'll just die! *(She exits. Ray-Bud returns to his seat beside Raynelle.)*

RAY-BUD.   Shouldn't be too much longer. You doing okay?

RAYNELLE.   Never better.

MARGUERITE.   *(Tapping Ray-Bud on the shoulder.)* When are we starting this thing?

RAY-BUD.   In a minute.

JUANITA.   Well, Suzanne, where's Junior?

SUZANNE.   How should I know? Ask Bernice Talbot.

JUANITA.   Oh, I'm sorry you're feeling so down in the dumps, Suzanne. You want some gum?

SUZANNE.   No, thanks.

JUANITA.   I always carry a pack of Juicy Fruit with me to weddings and funerals. Sort of gives me something to do while the preacher is talking. Yeah, I think it's something about the rhythm of it sort of lulls me. Helps my mind to wander. And do you know what I think about when my mind wanders?

SUZANNE.   I got a feeling you're gonna tell me.

JUANITA.   I think about my life. I think about the end of each day. How I tuck my precious little boy into bed, turn off the lights in my $400,000 home, slip into my beautiful black lace negligee, crawl into my king size bed, and lay there and wonder where the hell my husband is. You sure you don't want a piece?

SUZANNE.   Okay, I'll take one. Why don't you leave him?

JUANITA.   *(Laughs brightly.)* And go where? Suzanne, I'm not an unhappy person. Never said I was. I got everything I ever asked for.

SUZANNE.   But if he really loved you ...

JUANITA.   Then I might be forced into the God awful position of having to love him back. Do you love Junior?

SUZANNE.   I ... I ...

JUANITA.   Do you want him back? *(This time Suzanne opens her mouth, but nothing comes out. Juanita pats her hand, then settles back in her seat.)* You don't have to answer right now, Honey. Just sit back and let the Juicy Fruit take its effect. It'll come to you. *(Reverend Hooker enters with Lucille, who looks very embarrassed. Ray-Bud rises and he and Lucille take their seats in the front row opposite from Raynelle and Delightful.)*

REVEREND.   I'm sorry to keep everybody waiting. I had a real important phone call to make.

RAYNELLE.   *(To Ray-Bud.)* Told ya. *(To Reverend.)* We're real glad you could join us, Reverend.

REVEREND.   Thank you, Sister Turpin. Merline. *(He nods to the unseen organist. She begins to play.)* Before we begin, I'd like to thank our fine organist for maintaining the mood of our services while I was unavoidably detained. Our thanks to Sister Merline Depew. *(There is a sudden flourish in the music, sort of like a curtain call.)*

MARGUERITE.   You're not working at the skating rink, Merline.

REVEREND.   Well, shall we pray. *(Everyone bows their heads.)*

Heavenly father. *(Junior comes rushing in the door carrying a large paper bag and a somewhat smaller one.)*

JUNIOR. Sorry! Sorry I'm late. I just had to ... uh.... Y'all didn't bury him yet did you?

RAY-BUD. No, Junior. And at this rate, we never will. Now sit down! We're in the middle of a prayer here!

JUNIOR. Oh, sorry. *(He proceeds to find a seat with all eyes on him. He finally settles in beside Marguerite.)* Aunt Marguerite, could you just move your purse there. Yeah, okay. Okay. I'm fine. I'm fine. Sorry.

RAYNELLE. Go on, Reverend.

REVEREND. Shall we bow our heads. Heavenly Father, we come here today with heavy hearts, as we note with sadness the passing of our dearly departed, Bud Turpin. *(Junior begins digging around in one of the bags.)* Give peace to our hearts this day, Lord. Give us strength to face the new dawn. And guide us Lord through the long night. And help us to see the promise of a better tomorrow. *(Junior begins trying to attract Suzanne's attention. He pulls a paper covered straw out of the bag. Then tears off one end of the paper covering and blows into the straw sending the covering flying across the aisle at Suzanne, who ignores it.)*

JUNIOR. Psst!

SUZANNE. Stop it! *(The Reverend looks up. Junior and Suzanne quickly duck their heads.)*

REVEREND. *(Plowing ahead.)* Give peace to our hearts this day, Lord. Give us strength to face the new dawn. And guide us, Lord, through the long night. And help us to see the promise of a better tomorrow. *(Junior gets up, hurries down the aisle and places the small bag on the chair beside Suzanne, then hurries back to his seat. After a moment, she opens it and pulls out a plastic cup with the Dairy Queen logo on it. She looks over at Junior, who mouths the words "I love you." She looks blankly at him. His desperation rising, he mouths it again. She continues to stare at him.)* For what is yesterday, but the tomorrow we thought we couldn't face the day before. But with your help, we faced it. Just like we'll face today, tomorrow, and all our days to come, till you call us home to be with you and our beloved Brother Bud. Amen.

JUNIOR.   I LOVE YOU!

ROYCE.   Don't believe him, Suzanne. He told me the same thing.

SUZANNE.   Junior, what is this?

JUNIOR.   *(Nervously.)* A grape slush. *(Noting that all eyes are on him.)* And I got some Dilly Bars for the rest of you all.

SUZANNE.   You bought me a grape slush?

JUNIOR.   Yeah.

SUZANNE.   I LOVE YOU, JUNIOR!

JUNIOR.   I LOVE YOU TOO, SUZANNE! *(Junior and Suzanne race into each other's arms and kiss so passionately, they knock each other to the ground.)*

RAY-BUD.   ALRIGHT! THAT'S IT! THAT'S IT! GET UP! GET UP! GET IN THEM CHAIRS! GET IN THEM CHAIRS AND DON'T GET OUT OF 'EM! *(Junior and Suzanne quickly seat themselves next to Juanita.)*   NOW, IS THAT IT? ANYBODY HAVE ANYTHING ELSE THEY WANT TO SAY OR DO? EVERYBODY HAVE EVERYTHING THEY NEED? DELIGHT-FUL, WOULD YOU LIKE A DILLY BAR? *(Delightful nods enthusiastically.)* ALRIGHT, LET'S GET A DILLY BAR DOWN HERE! *(A Dilly Bar is passed down to Delightful.)* ANY-BODY ELSE? OKAY, THIS IS IT! I DON'T WANT TO HEAR ANOTHER WORD OUT OF ANYBODY! WE'RE DOING IT! WE'RE DOING IT COME HELL OR HIGH WATER! *(He sits.)* Alright, take it away, Reverend.

REVEREND.   Well, thank you, Ray. Now, I did not know Brother Turpin well, but to me he seemed a quiet man. A man of inner strength. A man who knew his own mind, kept his own counsel, and was at pea ... was at peace with the uh.... Peace with the uh.... Would you all excuse me for a minute? *(The Reverend exits quickly up the aisle. All heads follow him except Ray-Bud and Lucille who continue to face front. There is a long silence. The family members look to each other but nobody dares say a word. In the silence, Lucille begins to fight laughter. All eyes are now on Ray-Bud.)*

RAY-BUD.   He'll be back in a minute. Lucille would you mind to ... *(Their eyes meet. Lucille is about to explode.)* Lucille, are you laughing at my father's funeral? *(Lucille nods.)* Well

59

who the hell could blame you? *(Ray-Bud begins to laugh as well. They lose complete control, barely able to stay in their chairs. By this time, the other family members have taken notice. Some are standing to get a better look.)*

LUCILLE. I'm so sorry!

MARGUERITE. I can not believe it.

RAY-BUD. You see him run up that aisle?

LUCILLE. Yeah! *(They roar with laughter.)*

MARGUERITE. Bud, forgive your family for laughing in the funeral home.

RAYNELLE. I believe he does, Marguerite.

RAY-BUD. Lucille?

LUCILLE. Yeah?

RAY-BUD. I hate children!

LUCILLE. I thought you always wanted them!

RAY-BUD. You're all I ever wanted, Honey! *(They laugh even harder. Suddenly, Lucille stops.)*

LUCILLE. Ray-Bud, I got something to tell you. *(Marguerite crosses down to them.)*

MARGUERITE. Well, I hate to break up the party, but what are we gonna do now with no preacher?

RAYNELLE. We don't need no preacher. Ray, you get up there.

RAY-BUD. What?

RAYNELLE. You heard me. This is for us, Ray. We can take care of it ourselves. We don't need anybody's help. *(Calling off.)* Thank you, Merline, but this is a private service. Just family. *(There is an abrupt discord as Merline slams the lid of the organ.)* Go on, Ray. *(Ray-Bud moves slowly up to the podium. Everyone resumes their seats.)*

RAY-BUD. Well, I guess we come here today to pay our last respects. To say goodbye. Bud Turpin was a man who said ... what he said. And he did what he did. And he thought what he thought. And I don't know what any of that means to any of you all. But whatever it means. Whatever thought or feeling comes into your heart. Hold on to it. 'Cause that's what you got. That's what he left you. Good or bad. It's yours and nobody can ever take it away from you. *(Slight pause.)* And now we are truly lucky to have with us today, Mrs. Suzanne Marie Turpin, who has graciously consented to honor the memory of her father-in-law with a song. Suzanne.

SUZANNE.   *(Making her way to the front.)* Well, Ray, thank you. Uh ... well, it's been a long time since I sung in front of people. And of course I'm not real used to singing without accompaniment and all, but I'll ...

RAYNELLE.   *(Smiling sweetly.)* We're paying by the hour, Suzanne.

SUZANNE.   Oh! Yeah. Okay. *(She clears her throat and finds her pitch.)* Okay, I've got it. *(She begins. She sings with little talent, but great sincerity.)*

"There's a land that is fairer than day
And by faith we shall see it afar
For our father waits over the way
to prepare us a dwelling place there
(One by one, starting with Raynelle, the family members begin to stand and join her for the chorus. They harmonize as best they can.)
In the sweet bye and bye
we shall meet on that beautiful shore
In the sweet bye and bye
we shall meet on that beautiful shore"

(The lights change to isolate a small area at the front of the stage representing the casket. One by one, the family members move through this area as if they are viewing the body for the last time. The remaining family members continue to hum "In the Sweet Bye and Bye" throughout this section. Junior and Suzanne enter first.)

JUNIOR.   Well, Daddy. I know you always worried about us and the kids, but you don't have to anymore cause we got a plan for the future. Suzanne's gonna go into the music business and I'm gonna be her manager.

SUZANNE.   And we've decided we're gonna dedicate my first album to you. It's gonna be called "Songs of Love and Bud" and it's gonna have at least one song about an old man dying on a farm.

JUNIOR.   Keep your fingers crossed for us. *(They exit arm in arm. Ray-Bud and Lucille enter.)*

RAY-BUD.   Well, he sure looks peaceful, don't he?

LUCILLE.   Yes, he does.

MARGUERITE.   *(In darkness.)* Still looks kinda painted up to me.

LUCILLE.   Daddy Bud, about nine months from now we might just be getting a little surprise. And if it's a boy, we're gonna call him "Bud" and if it's a girl, we're gonna name her "Budeen." *(Lucille and Ray-Bud start to leave. Lucille leans back in confidentially.)* But don't get your hopes up. *(Ray-Bud and Lucille exit hand in hand. Marguerite and Royce enter)*

MARGUERITE.   Well, Royce, when I go, just put me out in a pine box. I don't want you spending a lot of money on me. Not that you'll have it.

ROYCE.   *(Placing a hand on her shoulder.)* Well, Mama, when the time comes just try to point your toes down like Uncle Bud did. That way I can just put you in the ground with a pile driver.

MARGUERITE.   You're a demon, Royce.

ROYCE.   Runs in the family, Mama. *(They exit. Raynelle with her arm around Delightful, steps into the light.)*

RAYNELLE.   Well, Honey you got anything you want to say to your Daddy.

DELIGHTFUL.   Bye.

RAYNELLE.   Well, short and sweet. Let me have a minute alone here, Honey. *(Delightful exits.)* Well, Bud, I guess this about wraps it up. I still wonder if you hid those scissors out of spite, but I guess I'll never know. I'll miss ya. But I don't want you to get your nose out of joint if I remarry. Take care of yourself. *(The humming stops.)* And Bud, save me a place. *(The light expands and the entire company moves into it. They sing the last line of the song in beautiful multi-part harmony. The final chord is resplendent, triumphant, and yes, happy.)* "WE SHALL MEET ... ON THAT BEAUTIFUL SHORE."

END OF PLAY

PROPERTY LIST

ACT ONE

Scene 1
Two chairs
Table
Handwritten letter (RAYNELLE)
Envelope (RAYNELLE
Coffee cup (BUD)

Scene 2
Wall telephone (MARGUERITE)
Wooden spoon (MARGUERITE
Sofa (used as Royce's bed)
Blanket (ROYCE)
Telephone (ROYCE)
Cigarettes (ROYCE)
Ash tray (ROYCE)
Lighter (ROYCE)

Scene 3
Table
Two chairs
Wall telephone
Note pad (LUCILLE)
Pencil (LUCILLE)
Coffee cup (RAY-BUD)
Sack lunch (LUCILLE)

Scene 4
Two chairs
Sheet music (SUZANNE)
Hand gun (JUNIOR)
Woman's earring (SUZANNE)

Scene 5
Table
Three chairs
Coffee cup
Bag of potato chips (DELIGHTFUL)
Note pad and pen (REVEREND)

Scene 6
Two chairs
Wrist watch (ROYCE)

Scene 7
Chairs
Sofa
Brochures
Tray of corndogs (LUCILLE)
Ice pack (SUZANNE)
Pills (LUCILLE)
Glass of water (LUCILLE)
Earring (Same as Scene 4) (SUZANNE)
Bible (MARGUERITE)
Note pad and pencil (RAY-BUD)
Purse (RAYNELLE)
Note pad and pencil (RAYNELLE)
Money (RAYNELLE)

Scene 8
Step unit (or bench)
Liquor bottle (RAY-BUD)
Drinking glass (JUNIOR)

Scene 9
Chair
Table
Microphone (on table)
Microphone with stand (JOY OF LIFE SINGERS)
Notes (REVEREND)

ACT TWO

Scene 1
    Chairs
    Table (used to represent casket)
    Purse (MARGUERITE)
    Handkerchief (MARGUERITE)
    Instamatic camera with flash (MARGUERITE)
    Bubble gum (DELIGHTFUL)
    Coca-Cola (JUNIOR)

Scene 2
    Three chairs
    Large purse (VEDA)
    Pill box (VEDA)
    Pills (VEDA)
    Small tank of oxygen (VEDA)
    Oxygen mask with tubing (VEDA)
    Package of crackers (VEDA)

Scene 3
    Two chairs
    Doll (to represent baby) (NADINE)
    Baby blanket (NADINE)
    Diaper bag (NADINE)
    Wallet (NADINE)
    Long string of photos (NADINE)

Scene 4
    Can of beer (CLYDE)

Scene 5
    Two chairs
    Paper towel (ROYCE)

Scene 6

Chair
Table
Tablecloth
Paper plates
Plastic forks
Various covered dishes or casseroles
Package of M&Ms (DELIGHTFUL)
Bag of potato chips
Brown paper sack
Bucket of Kentucky Fried Chicken

Scene 7

Bed
Shirts
Pair of bedroom slippers (RAYNELLE)
Paper bag
Purse (RAYNELLE)
Scissors (RAYNELLE)

Scene 8

Chairs
Pack of Juicy Fruit Gum (JUANITA)
Large plain white paper bag (JUNIOR)
Smaller plain white paper bag (JUNIOR)
Paper covered drinking straw (JUNIOR)
Small plastic cup with top (JUNIOR)

I HAVE THE JOY

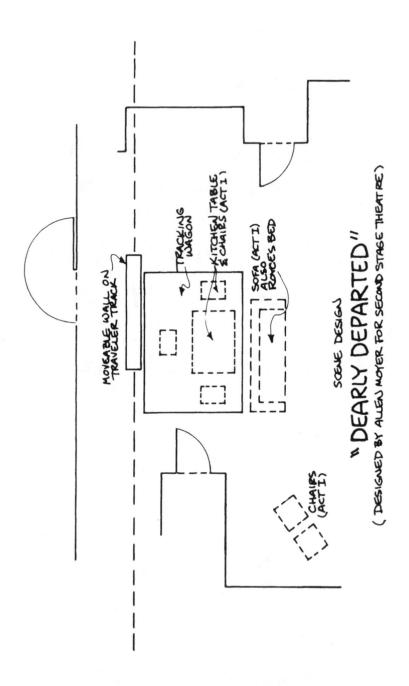

MOVEABLE WALL ON TRAVELER TRACK

TRACKING WAGON

KITCHEN TABLE & CHAIRS (ACT I)

SOFA (ACT I) ALSO ROYCE'S BED

CHAIRS (ACT I)

SCENE DESIGN

"DEARLY DEPARTED"

(DESIGNED BY ALLEN MOYER FOR SECOND STAGE THEATRE)

NEW PLAYS

★ **BENGAL TIGER AT THE BAGHDAD ZOO by Rajiv Joseph.** The lives of two American Marines and an Iraqi translator are forever changed by an encounter with a quick-witted tiger who haunts the streets of war-torn Baghdad. "[A] boldly imagined, harrowing and surprisingly funny drama." *–NY Times.* "Tragic yet darkly comic and highly imaginative." *–CurtainUp.* [5M, 2W] ISBN: 978-0-8222-2565-2

★ **THE PITMEN PAINTERS by Lee Hall, inspired by a book by William Feaver.** Based on the triumphant true story, a group of British miners discover a new way to express themselves and unexpectedly become art-world sensations. "Excitingly ambiguous, in-the-moment theater." *–NY Times.* "Heartfelt, moving and deeply politicized." *–Chicago Tribune.* [5M, 2W] ISBN: 978-0-8222-2507-2

★ **RELATIVELY SPEAKING by Ethan Coen, Elaine May and Woody Allen.** In TALKING CURE, Ethan Coen uncovers the sort of insanity that can only come from family. Elaine May explores the hilarity of passing in GEORGE IS DEAD. In HONEYMOON MOTEL, Woody Allen invites you to the sort of wedding day you won't forget. "Firecracker funny." *–NY Times.* "A rollicking good time." *–New Yorker.* [8M, 7W] ISBN: 978-0-8222-2394-8

★ **SONS OF THE PROPHET by Stephen Karam.** If to live is to suffer, then Joseph Douaihy is more alive than most. With unexplained chronic pain and the fate of his reeling family on his shoulders, Joseph's health, sanity, and insurance premium are on the line. "Explosively funny." *–NY Times.* "At once deep, deft and beautifully made." *–New Yorker.* [5M, 3W] ISBN: 978-0-8222-2597-3

★ **THE MOUNTAINTOP by Katori Hall.** A gripping reimagination of events the night before the assassination of the civil rights leader Dr. Martin Luther King, Jr. "An ominous electricity crackles through the opening moments." *–NY Times.* "[A] thrilling, wild, provocative flight of magical realism." *–Associated Press.* "Crackles with theatricality and a humanity more moving than sainthood." *–NY Newsday.* [1M, 1W] ISBN: 978-0-8222-2603-1

★ **ALL NEW PEOPLE by Zach Braff.** Charlie is 35, heartbroken, and just wants some time away from the rest of the world. Long Beach Island seems to be the perfect escape until his solitude is interrupted by a motley parade of misfits who show up and change his plans. "Consistently and sometimes sensationally funny." *–NY Times.* "A morbidly funny play about the trendy new existential condition of being young, adorable, and miserable." *–Variety.* [2M, 2W] ISBN: 978-0-8222-2562-1

DRAMATISTS PLAY SERVICE, INC.
440 Park Avenue South, New York, NY 10016   212-683-8960   Fax 212-213-1539
postmaster@dramatists.com   www.dramatists.com

NEW PLAYS

★ **CLYBOURNE PARK by Bruce Norris.** WINNER OF THE 2011 PULITZER PRIZE AND 2012 TONY AWARD. Act One takes place in 1959 as community leaders try to stop the sale of a home to a black family. Act Two is set in the same house in the present day as the now predominantly African-American neighborhood battles to hold its ground. "Vital, sharp-witted and ferociously smart." *–NY Times.* "A theatrical treasure…Indisputably, uproariously funny." *–Entertainment Weekly.* [4M, 3W] ISBN: 978-0-8222-2697-0

★ **WATER BY THE SPOONFUL by Quiara Alegría Hudes.** WINNER OF THE 2012 PULITZER PRIZE. A Puerto Rican veteran is surrounded by the North Philadelphia demons he tried to escape in the service. "This is a very funny, warm, and yes uplifting play." *–Hartford Courant.* "The play is a combination poem, prayer and app on how to cope in an age of uncertainty, speed and chaos." *–Variety.* [4M, 3W] ISBN: 978-0-8222-2716-8

★ **RED by John Logan.** WINNER OF THE 2010 TONY AWARD. Mark Rothko has just landed the biggest commission in the history of modern art. But when his young assistant, Ken, gains the confidence to challenge him, Rothko faces the agonizing possibility that his crowning achievement could also become his undoing. "Intense and exciting." *–NY Times.* "Smart, eloquent entertainment." *–New Yorker.* [2M] ISBN: 978-0-8222-2483-9

★ **VENUS IN FUR by David Ives.** Thomas, a beleaguered playwright/director, is desperate to find an actress to play Vanda, the female lead in his adaptation of the classic sadomasochistic tale *Venus in Fur.* "Ninety minutes of good, kinky fun." *–NY Times.* "A fast-paced journey into one man's entrapment by a clever, vengeful female." *–Associated Press.* [1M, 1W] ISBN: 978-0-8222-2603-1

★ **OTHER DESERT CITIES by Jon Robin Baitz.** Brooke returns home to Palm Springs after a six-year absence and announces that she is about to publish a memoir dredging up a pivotal and tragic event in the family's history—a wound they don't want reopened. "Leaves you feeling both moved and gratify-ingly sated." *–NY Times.* "A genuine pleasure." *–NY Post.* [2M, 3W] ISBN: 978-0-8222-2605-5

★ **TRIBES by Nina Raine.** Billy was born deaf into a hearing family and adapts brilliantly to his family's unconventional ways, but it's not until he meets Sylvia, a young woman on the brink of deafness, that he finally understands what it means to be understood. "A smart, lively play." *–NY Times.* "[A] bright and boldly provocative drama." *–Associated Press.* [3M, 2W] ISBN: 978-0-8222-2751-9

DRAMATISTS PLAY SERVICE, INC.
440 Park Avenue South, New York, NY 10016 212-683-8960 Fax 212-213-1539
postmaster@dramatists.com www.dramatists.com